MADAME DE STAËL

TWAYNE'S WORLD AUTHORS SERIES

A Survey of the World's Literature

Sylvia E. Bowman, Indiana University

GENERAL EDITOR

FRANCE

Maxwell A. Smith, Guerry Professor of French, Emeritus
The University of Chattanooga
Visiting Professor in Modern Languages
The Florida State University

EDITOR

Madame de Staël

(TWAS 69)

TWAYNE'S WORLD AUTHORS SERIES (TWAS)

The purpose of TWAS is to survey the major writers —novelists, dramatists, historians, poets, philosophers, and critics—of the nations of the world. Among the national literatures covered are those of Australia, Canada, China, Eastern Europe, France, Germany, Greece, India, Italy, Japan, Latin America, New Zealand, Poland, Russia, Scandinavia, Spain, and the African nations, as well as Hebrew, Yiddish, and Latin Classical literatures. This survey is complemented by Twayne's United States Authors Series and English Authors Series.

The intent of each volume in these series is to present a critical-analytical study of the works of the writer; to include biographical and historical material that may be necessary for understanding, appreciation, and critical appraisal of the writer; and to present all material in clear, concise English—but not to vitiate the scholarly content of the work by doing so.

Madame de Staël

By Helen B. Posgate

Twayne Publishers, Inc.   ::   New York

Acknowledgments

I would like here to acknowledge gratefully permission to quote from the following publishers: The Bobbs-Merrill Company, Inc., *Mistress to an Age,* by Christopher Herold; Doubleday and Company, Inc., *Madame de Staël on Politics, Literature and National Character,* by Morroe Berger; The University of Michigan Press, *France,* by Albert Guerard; Astra Books, *Madame de Staël and Freedom Today,* by Nixon and Forsberg.

I am glad to acknowledge also the cooperation of Trinity College Library, Hartford, Connecticut, which kindly borrowed books from the Yale University Library for my research.

I am personally indebted to Mrs. Lucy Beers, to Mrs. Dorothy S. Jones, to Dr. Maxwell A. Smith, and to my husband for technical and critical assistance in the preparation of this fascinating subject.

Hartford, Connecticut

Preface

Since neither the character nor the works of Madame de Staël can be properly understood without reference to the historical background, I have included a sketch of the times and a chronology. I have not entered into the complex details. That task is for the historian. Many times I have let Mme de Staël tell the story of events herself, since she and her family were personally involved in them.

Other writers have taken up the personal details of her love life at some length. I share the opinion of Forsberg and Nixon that "The private habits of Ulysses S. Grant should not becloud the historical evaluation of Lee's surrender at Appomattox, and one needs no photograph of Columbus to explain the significance of his discovery of America." Stephen Spender also has pointed out, in the *Saturday Review* (Jan. 15, 1964), the danger that the revelation of the imperfect life of a writer will detract from the reader's appreciation.

The eighteenth century was famous for its brilliant and corrupt society. A strict morality would have relegated Mme de Staël to a position as a domestic nonentity of which her passionate nature could not conceive. She had been brought up in the midst of the exciting discussions of the philosophic ideas of liberty and social reform in her mother's *salon*. There she came to know, at a very young age, the men and ideas of the Enlightenment. Her passionate, sensitive nature, her intellectual superiority, could never have succumbed to the level of the conventional limitations imposed on the women of her day. Her way of life, moreover, was for her time not exceptional among women of note. It was her political influence which made her remarkable.

That she sought in vain her ideal of the perfect love, which alone could give happiness, was the result of her own nature, as well as of her upbringing. We must know her as the firm advocate of liberty, as the opponent of despotism, as the strong influence for constitutional government. We must realize her achievement in opening the narrow doors of nationalism, in interpreting eighteenth-century ideas, in influencing literary criticism as well as leading into the romantic nineteenth century with her ideal of enthusiasm. Madame de Staël presents to us one of the most fascinating characters in one of the most exciting eras of European history.

I hope this presentation of her life and times will provide much food for thought for the modern student of French literature and culture. I have made an effort to leave the student free to form his own judgment of her ideas and influence.

HELEN B. POSGATE

Contents

MADAME DE STAËL

by

HELEN B. POSGATE

This volume provides an examination of the works of Madame de Staël, one of the more thoughtful European writers of the early nineteenth century. As member of the French aristocracy, she found refuge in England during the Reign of Terror in France. Holding to her faith in the perfectibility of man, in the power of enlightened thought to lift man above the morass of violence, selfishness, and hatred, her voice was constantly raised against all forms of fanaticism. She spoke for tolerance, love, and humanity, and against despotism and corruption in government. She held great ideas to be indestructible, and believed them to be the property of all nations.

Madame de Staël gave new meaning to the words "Classic" and "Romantic." Literature in her eyes was not only a great civilizing force — a source of comfort to the depressed and discouraged — but also an important influence on political institutions. Her great books, *Of Literature, Germany,* and *Considerations on the Principal Events of the French Revolution,* stand as examples of international thinking.

Chronology

Madame de Staël

1766 Anne Louise Germaine Necker born April 22.

1767 Jacques Necker, father, Minister of Republic of Geneva to French court of Louis XVI.

1778– Necker Minister of Finance.
81

1781 Necker's *Compte-Rendu* and exile.

1786 Marriage of Germaine to Eric Magnus de Staël-Holstein, Swedish Ambassador in Paris.

1787 July 31. Germaine's baby, Edwige-Gustavine, born; lived only twenty months.

1786– *Sophie, ou les Sentiments Secrets Jane Gray* (published
87 1795). Nouvelles: *Mirza, Adélaïde et Théodore, Pauline.*

1788 *Lettres sur les Ecrits et le Caractère de Jean-Jacques Rousseau.* Liaison with Louis de Narbonne.

1790 Aug. 31. Birth of Auguste de Staël.

1792 Aug. 10. Mme de Staël saves Narbonne and other liberal aristocrats, who escape to England.

Sept. to Jan. Retires to Coppet.

Nov. 20. Birth of Albert, second son.

Jan. Mme de Staël goes to England to join Narbonne and group of *émigrés.* Rents Juniper Hall for three months.

March. Forced to return to Coppet; Narbonne remains in England.

1793– Mme de Staël organizes rescue of friends from the Terror.
96

1794 Writes *Zulma; Reflections on Peace* (to Pitt).

1795 *Reflections on Internal Peace.* Publishes *Mirza, Pauline, Adélaïde et Théodore, Essay on Fiction.* Exiled from Paris by Directory.

1796 *Influence of the Passions on Individuals and Nations.*

Chronology

1797 June 8. Albertine de Staël is born.
Dec. 6. Mme de Staël first meets Bonaparte.

1800 *De la Littérature.* Jan. 4. Mme de Staël begins opposition to Napoleon. Separation from Baron de Staël.

1802 May 8. Baron de Staël dies en route to Coppet.

1803 *Delphine.* Oct. 24. Mme de Staël goes to Germany, visits with Goethe, Schiller, and other writers. Wm. Schlegel returns with her as tutor.

1804 April 9. Necker, her beloved father, dies. Dec. to June, 1805, trip to Italy. Germaine works on notes for *Germany* (*De l'Allemagne*). Many visitors; dramatic performances.

1805–7 Many short trips into France.

1807 Publication of Mme de Staël's *Corinne;* Constant's *Adolphe.* Short trip to Germany and Austria.

1808 Interest in mysticism at Coppet. Apr. to Oct., 1810 spent at Chaumont.

1810 First version of *De l'Allemagne* (*Germany*); Destroyed by order of Napoleon. Sept. Order of exile to Coppet. Dec. Meets John Rocca who falls in love with her.

1811 May. Secret marriage with Rocca.

1812 April 7. "Little-Us," Louis Alphonse Rocca, is born.
Apr. 23. Mme de Staël and family escape from Coppet on journey to Sweden via Russia. Sept. Arrives in Stockholm, remains to May.

1813 May. She goes to England; death of Albert in duel with Cossack. Death of Narbonne. *Reflections on Suicide* published.

1814 May. Mme de Staël returns to Paris; to Coppet in July. Recovery of Necker's loan of two million francs. Marriage of Albertine and Victor de Broglie in Italy.

1816 Public marriage with John Rocca.

1817 July 14. Death of Mme de Staël in Paris. Posthumous publication of *Ten Years of Exile* and *Considerations on the Principal Events of the French Revolution.*

French Historical Background

1776 Necker, Contrôleur Général des Finances.

1781 Exile of Necker to Coppet, Switzerland.

1787 Feb. 22. First Assembly of Notables at Versailles.

1788 Sept. Necker again Minister.
      Nov. Second Assembly of Notables.
1789 May 5. Meeting of States General at Versailles.
      June 17. Becomes National Assembly.
      June 20. Oath of the Tennis Court.
      June 27. Union of the Three Orders, National Assembly.
      July 11. Necker dismissed.
      July 14. Fall of the Bastille.
      July 24. Necker recalled to Ministry.
      Aug. 4. By Decree of Assembly, abolition of privileges and feudal rights in France.
      Oct. 5-6. March of Paris populace on Versailles.
      Nov. 2. Church lands declared national property.
1790 Feb. 13. Suppression of Religious Orders.
      July 14. Anniversary of Fall of Bastille.
      Sept. 14. Resignation of Necker.
1791 June 21. Attempted flight of Louis XVI.
      Aug. 27. Convention of Pilnitz.
      Sept. 14. Louis accepts the Constitution.
      Oct. 1. Legislative Assembly.
1792 Mar. 29. Gustavus III of Sweden assassinated.
      Apr. 20. France declares war on Austria.
      June 20. Insurrection of Paris suburbs. Red bonnet placed on Louis' head.
      July 14. Oath of Federation—3rd Bastille Anniversary.
      Aug. 10. Insurrection in Paris; massacre of Swiss Guards in Tuileries; suspension of King's power.
      Sept. 21. Opening of National Convention. Republic is proclaimed.
1793 Jan. 21. Trial and execution of Louis XVI.
      Feb. 1. War declared on England and Holland.
      Apr. 6. Committee of Public Safety.
      May 31. Reign of Terror begins.
      June 24. New Constitution of 1793 presented.
      Oct. 6. New French Calendar.
      Oct. 25. Execution of Marie Antoinette.
1794 July 27. Fall of Robespierre; Terror ends.
1795 Peace between France, Prussia, Spain.
      Aug. 22. New Constitution; executive power vested in Directory.

Oct. 25. New legislature: 1. Council of Ancients. 2. Council of 500.

1796 Mar. 30. Bonaparte commander in Italy; success of his armies.

1798 May. Expedition to Egypt.

1799 April to Sept. Successes of Allies against the French.

Oct. 16. Bonaparte arrives from Egypt.

Nov. 9. Coup d'état; Napoleon made Consul.

1800 French success under Napoleon and his generals.

1802 Aug. 2. Napoleon declared Consul for life.

1803 May 16. War on England.

1804 Mar. 21. Execution of Duc d'Enghien.

May 18. Napoleon becomes Emperor.

Dec. 2. Crowned by Pope in Paris.

1805 Apr. 11. Third Coalition of Allies against France.

Oct. 21. Battle of Trafalgar.

1806 Napoleon's victories.

Nov. 21. His sea blockade.

1807 More victories.

1808 Apr. to

1809 Jan. War in Spain.

1810 Jan. 9. Marriage of Napoleon and Josephine annulled.

Apr. 1. Marriage to Marie Louise of Austria.

1811 Napoleon's son is born; King of Rome.

1812 June 22. War declared on Russia.

Oct. 19. French armies evacuate Moscow.

Nov. 28. Passage of the Beresina; total loss of the French Army.

1813 More battles of Napoleon in Germany.

Oct. 16-18. Battle of Leipzig and Hanau; French withdraw.

1814 Jan. Allies invade France.

Mar. 31. Paris is occupied.

Apr. 1. Napoleon abdicates; is sent to Elba.

1815 "The Hundred Days."

March 6. Napoleon returns.

June 18. Battle of Waterloo.

Napoleon sent to St. Helena.

Louis XVIII placed at head of Government.

CHAPTER 1

Historical Background

To understand Madame de Staël's life it is well first to understand the times in which she lived. The famous politician
and friend of Mme de Staël, Talleyrand, an archetype of the
gentlemen of the Enlightenment, remarked that those who had
never known this period were ignorant of the sweetness of living.
Refinement and politeness were the rule in the aristocratic society
that developed the art of living as a fine art.

Rules and conventions of conduct were established, recognized,
and practiced. Woe to those who dared to ignore or to rise
above them! The art of conversation, of repartee, and gallant
speech characterized all the social gatherings, where the influence of beautiful women was prominent. "Conversation in
France," wrote Mme de Staël, "is an instrument on which they
are fond of playing and which animates the spirit like music
among some people, and strong liquor among others."[1] The
French were characterized by their wit. It could be cruel at
times and even malicious.

French culture of the eighteenth century was much admired
and even imitated abroad. Men of culture from all countries of
Europe made long visits to Paris. Frederick II wrote verses in
French and had Voltaire correct them. Catherine II of Russia
invited Diderot to her court.

French art, both painting and sculpture, was well-known in
Europe. Paintings by Watteau and Fragonard could be found
in foreign courts. Mme de Staël sat for a portrait by Mme
Vigée-LeBrun. Houdon, the sculptor, did a famous statue of
Voltaire, as well as one of George Washington, and busts of
Franklin, Jefferson, and La Fayette. Gardens in the French style
were to be found everywhere.

Above all, the century was known for its spirit of inquiry and
research as well as for its satirical criticism. Names, such as

Diderot and D'Alembert, the Encyclopedists, and in the sciences, Réaumur (thermometer), Lavoisier (chemistry), Condorcet (mathematics), and Buffon, the naturalist, are examples of this scientific interest. It was in 1783 that the first ascension by balloon was made by the Montgolfier brothers.

The chief characteristic of the century was its interest in ideas; these ideas attacked the old traditions and the old *régime*. Jean-Jacques Rousseau challenged the old ideas of government and education in his *Contrat Social* and *Emile*, pleading the cause of the individual against society.

People were no longer willing to accept the domination of the upper class. Men began to think and to discuss their rights and such abstract ideas as equality and liberty. Even the theater was penetrated by the new spirit of criticism. Beaumarchais's *Le Mariage de Figaro* (1784) presented a man of the Third Estate protesting against the privileged society of birth and wealth. Marivaux's comedies provided light entertainment for this society that abhorred boredom. Many of the liberal aristocrats and clergy applauded their protest against the status quo and sympathized with the movement to correct the old abuses.

In addition to the strong influence of Voltaire and Rousseau there stood another important thinker whose work was to penetrate the thought of Mme de Staël. This was Montesquieu, who had made a visit to England. His interest was the study of governments. His book *The Spirit of Laws* (*L'Esprit des Lois*) presented such ideas as the influence of climate, geography, religion, and customs on government. Although he favored a monarchical government for France, he laid down the principle of the separation of the three powers, the executive, the legislative, and the judicial, and he praised the English form of constitutional law.

But what of the daily life of the society in which Mme de Staël was brought up? Lady Blennerhasset gives an eloquent description of the mentality of the early revolutionary days:

When the Revolution broke out it was headed by noblemen who were ready to speak and to fight, priests who could organize, bishops who could bless, princes who could pay for it, and a king who could allow it to happen. Nothing was too venturesome for this race. Everything might be said or done if only the manner of doing it were correct, pleasing and piquant.[2]

This correct, pleasing, and piquant manner was manifested in the famous *salons* of the century: those of Mme Geoffrin for artists and literary men; of Mme du Deffant, her rival, for the Encyclopedists; of Mlle de Lespinasse, Mme d'Holbach and Mme d'Helvétius where free speech reigned. To this series of *salons* was added the *salon* of Mme Necker not long after her marriage in 1764. It was in her *salon* that she promoted the career of her husband Jacques Necker, who became Contrôleur Général des Finances for Louis XVI. It was there that her daughter Germaine listened to, and absorbed, the ideas of such visitors as Grimm, Diderot, D'Alembert, Buffon, Marmontel, the Abbés Raynal, Galiani, and Morellet.

Madame Necker, strict Calvinist as she was, presided over a strange assemblage of irreligious, libertine philosophers. To quote Herold:

They were the press, they were public opinion, they were the teachers of kings; no single group of intellectuals ever held such power before or since.[3]

The *salons* were the kingdom of conversation, and the subjects discussed were literature, art, politics, and current happenings. Authors sometimes read their latest works there; it was the scepter that ruled supreme. Criticism, serious criticism, was expressed lightly, gaily, but the undercurrent was at times bitter and destructive.

Elaborate balls with much dancing and gaming occupied the aristocratic society. The ladies wore elaborate gowns, and their headdresses were at times spectacular. Fashion and novelty set the tone of society. Court life was a dizzy round of dinners, balls, and entertainments, as Mme de Staël discovered when wife of the Swedish Ambassador. Dueling was common.

This gay, witty, and charming society, with its powdered, showy, intelligent men of the world and its ladies of fashion and clever tongue, was destined to a tragic death in the French Revolution. The role of Mme de Staël in the Revolution was a significant one. Of that role Lady Blennerhasset wrote, "She was a spiritual link in the chain of a great deliverance, and with masculine courage she imparted the liberal opinions she had preserved through twelve years . . . of struggle to the France of later years."4

Mme de Staël's life (1766-1817) covered fifty years of the greatest changes in social, political, philosophic, and literary thought of modern times. She was a vital and significant force in those changes. Those were the days of the French and American Revolutions. Her father, Jacques Necker, played an official role in the French government under Louis XVI. Today, about one hundred and fifty years after her death, her ideas still ring true as clarion calls to freedom and civil rights.

Various Appraisals of Mme de Staël

Since 1900 there have been many books about her. Countless magazine articles in numerous countries have been written on the many phases of her thought and influence. Her character and life have been portrayed from many different points of view. To one she is a brilliant, spoiled child of the eighteenth century; to another, the great interpreter of Europe and especially of Germany to France; to another, an unprincipled, unconventional female, meddling in government and politics for personal glory.

It is interesting to note the contradictory appreciations of Mme de Staël's character by some of those who knew her personally. Madame de Charrière, a disillusioned woman and an unfriendly critic, called her "a talking machine." In his early infatuation Benjamin Constant wrote, "Her mind dazzled me, her gaiety enchanted me, her praise turned my head." He later protested against the domination of the "Man-woman."

Madame de Boufflers, who helped De Staël engineer his marriage to Germaine, judged the youthful Germaine severely. "She is so persuaded of her own superiority that it will be difficult to draw her attention to what she lacks. She is obstinate and domineering, and possesses an assurance such as I have never come across in any society, or in any woman of her age."

Her cousin, Mme Necker de Saussure, who wrote her first biography, reminds us that in matters of religion her uppermost thought was that of Christian morality. Her own life did not serve as a model, and she was the first to confess it. Friendship to Mme de Staël meant a sacred and enduring relationship. In spite of the persecution she suffered, she never harbored personal hatred or bitterness. She illustrated compassion and benevolence in her courageous rescue work during the Reign of Terror.

Lacretelle, who visited the Neckers in 1802, wrote:

The man who should murmur against her lack of beauty would fall at her feet dazzled by her intellect. She was born an intellectual conqueror.

After her visit to Germany Goethe wrote:

We must realize that she was a woman of tremendous influence. She drove a breach in the Chinese wall of prejudices that separated us from France, so that we grew to be appreciated not only across the Rhine, but even across the Channel.

Schiller's comment is frank and friendly, writing to Goethe:

She is all of one piece, and there isn't any single false note or pathological trait in her nature. . . . She stands for French culture in all its simplicity, and she casts an interesting light on the subject. As far as philosophy is concerned, particularly in the noblest sense of the word, we'll never understand each other, no matter how long the conversation lasts. But her instincts are better than her metaphysics, and her intellect, which is first-rate, is capable of rising to certain heights. She wants to explain everything; she wants to examine everything and she wants to pass judgment on everything. She can't conceive of any dark or intangible forces, and what she can't light up with her torch might just as well not exist.

Byron, who knew her personally, said, "She thought like a man, but alas she felt like a woman."

Sainte-Beuve, who often commented on her, wrote in his *Portraits de Femmes*:

Artist in a high degree through *Corinne*, Madame de Staël remains eminent in her other phases, namely as political thinker, moralist, critic and writer of memoires. Her place in posterity was sealed by the publication of her *Considerations on the Principal Events of the French Revolution*.

The variety of comments on her indicate the many facets of

her character and her work. Maurice Levaillant in the Prologue to his *The Passionate Exiles* felt that she epitomized twenty years of French history.

She symbolized one of its essential aspects. Whereas everything had yielded to the glory with which the Emperor had eventually succeeded in crushing France, she had resisted its glitter; at enormous cost to herself she had defended the rights of the spirit, of sentiment, of poetry, and, in a word, of liberty. In the political, as in the literary sphere, she had worked for the advent of a regime and a state of opinion, the triumph of which was promised by the Restoration, though still rather diffidently.

She has been called "The feminine de Tocqueville."

Margaret Goldsmith entitled her book *Portrait of a Liberal in the Revolutionary Age.*

She was one of the first independent political women who, unlike her predecessors, did not exert her influence from the intimate apartment of a King or some other powerful individual, but made herself felt through her intelligence, her personality, her books and her *salon.*

To simplify these varied estimates of Mme de Staël we can speak of the dualism of her character. She was both intellect and heart. Her keen intellect possessed remarkable qualities of observation and analysis. Thus she developed, through her study of history of literature and government, her recurring themes of man's perfectibility, of his civil rights, and of his freedom. Through her heart she emphasized the immense value of enthusiasm, feeling, benevolence, and toleration. She stood at the door that was closing on the eighteenth and already opening on the Romantic nineteenth century. Her struggle in behalf of the rights of the individual gives her new life today.

Parental Background

To understand the life and works of Germaine it is well to know something of the father she worshiped and of the mother she resembled in many ways. Her mother, Suzanne Curchod, was the daughter of a Protestant pastor in the village of Crassnier, in the canton of Vaud, Switzerland. The family was poor, but Suzanne's mother gave her an outstanding education in Latin,

Greek, mathematics, and the natural sciences. Suzanne played
the harpsichord and the violin. She dabbled in painting and, in
addition, she was a beautiful girl with wit and intelligence. A
circle of admirers formed around her, not only in her own
village, but in nearby Lausanne, which she often visited, and
where she was a member of a group of young people that called
itself the "Academy of Waters."

Here she danced and enjoyed the admiration of the young
men. She even became president of the Academy and loved the
discussions of such topics as "Can the same kind of friendship
exist between a man and a woman as between two men or two
women?" and "Which of all the pleasures is the most delicate?"[5]
She was a favorite for her gaiety, but she held off her admirers
of which she had many. She had a strong sense of her own
worth and definite ambitions, and aspired to a marriage with a
man who might satisfy them.

In June, 1757, Suzanne met Edward Gibbon in Lausanne, sent
there by his father to study and to think over his "escapade into
Catholicism." Suzanne was captivated by his mental talents and
good birth, which in her eyes set him above the men she knew.
Gibbon had already heard of the charms and beauty of Mlle
Curchod and watched her appreciatively as she danced at the
social gatherings of Lausanne. They were both twenty and fell
in love with each other. For Suzanne this experience was an
intellectual one, tinged with youthful passion. Gibbon's physical
appearance—he had pudgy cheeks and bags under his eyes—was
counterbalanced by his brilliant conversation, lively spirits, and
gentlemanly manners. He would certainly make his name known
in the world.

Their engagement was an informal one, which Gibbon unfortunately forgot to mention to his father in England. In April,
1758, his father sent for him to come home. For four months
Gibbon apparently did not bring up the subject of his French
engagement. When he did, the elder Gibbon, in no uncertain
terms, told his son that if he married this foreigner he would
have only his income of £300 per annum, and would be sending
him prematurely to his grave. As an Englishman he would be
trampling under foot his sacred duties. The result: "I sighed as
a lover, I obeyed as a son."[6]

In August he wrote Suzanne his letter of farewell and went

on to enjoy the pleasures of English town life. Nearly six years later he returned to Lausanne to share the merry round of social life with other Englishmen while he pursued his studies that later culminated in his great work, *The Decline and Fall of the Roman Empire.* Suzanne's letter at this time asked him to set her mind at peace that her soul might be reconciled "to its fate." Gibbon responded with an offer of friendship, nothing more.

These were difficult times for Suzanne. Her father had died in 1760, and Suzanne was obliged to work to support herself and her mother. She gave private lessons to children of good families but vented her inner bitterness and frustration upon her ailing mother. When the latter died in 1763, Suzanne was overcome with remorse and self-reproach, which she carried throughout her life. A friend, Pastor Moultou, took her into his home, where she taught his children. Through him she met Voltaire whom they visited every Saturday at nearby Ferney, and also Jean-Jacques Rousseau, who was a friend of Moultou, her protector.

During this period of anguish over her mother's death and Gibbon's coldness, she threw herself into the gay whirl of society in Lausanne. A critic has seen in this frantic social life of Suzanne the same ambiguous character later revealed in her daughter, Germaine, the self-dramatization of a hypersensitive personality. To Gibbon, Suzanne simply appeared insincere. She was at the same time corresponding with a Monsieur Correvon, a lawyer of Yverdon, but Suzanne held him off, waiting for something better to come her way, as come it did.

In 1764 a pretty young widow, Mme de Vermenoux, went to Geneva to consult the fashionable doctor of the day, Dr. Tronchin. She took lodgings with Pastor Moultou. When she was to return to Paris she would need a tutor for her eight-year-old son and a companion for herself. Suzanne accepted her offer, and they went to Paris in June.

It happened that Jacques Necker, a Paris banker who was seeking a wife, was then attentive to Mme Vermenoux, but she regarded him without encouragement. He turned to Suzanne, who had her cap set for him, and they were married a few months later.

Jacques Necker

Jacques Necker was a Pomeranian by birth, of an obscure family of Lutheran pastors.[7] His father had risen from this background to become tutor to the son of the Elector of Hanover's chief minister. The Elector became George I of England. As a result, Karl Friedrich Necker received an appointment to direct a boarding school for young Englishmen in Geneva. He was made professor of public law for his services, a very important title in the highly rigid class system of the Republic of Geneva, and was granted citizenship rights. The same year he married Jeanne Gautier, daughter of the First Syndic of the Republic. (To us this would probably mean the mayor.)

Two sons were born, Louis and Jacques. Jacques was trained in law but left school at the age of fifteen and became clerk in the banking house of Isaac Vernet.[8] There he made good and three years later was transferred to Paris. By nature deliberate, frugal, steady, and honest, he was not attracted by the gay life of the Parisian gaming tables and actresses' dressing rooms. He applied himself diligently to the making of money, and he was very successful. To the financier the field for speculation on government securities and grain prices was an attractive one in the eighteenth century. France had no banking system of her own, as the taking of interest was still under the ban of the Church.

It was with the Paris branches of the Protestant banking houses that modern French finance originated. Among these, the Dutch and Genevese were foremost. Given the opportunities of the time, every shaveling errand boy in a Genevese bank was a potential Rothschild.[9] Necker made his first millions through a judicious purchase and sale of French and English treasury bonds, but there is no doubt that he was perfectly honest in all his dealings. At the age of thirty-two he assumed sole direction of the Bank of Thélusson in Paris; he was then worth several million francs.

By this time he realized his need to establish himself socially and looked to marriage to accomplish this. It was while he was courting the attractive but undecided widow, Mme de Vermenoux, that he met and decided to marry her companion, Suzanne Curchod, whose reputation he had taken the trouble to investigate on a trip to Switzerland.

Suzanne was tall, blonde, well educated, and a Protestant. She performed every duty methodically and according to rules, but her inner soul was passionate and ambitious. Later at the French court she was called, "a governess who must have been soaked in a bucket of starch."[10]

Suzanne and Jacques went to live in a large but unfashionable house in the Marais section of Paris, near his business office. She worshiped her husband, and together they presented the picture of married happiness and fidelity, a model not very common in the Paris society of that day. Madame Necker centered all her ambitious life-interest in her husband.

Birth of Germaine

Anne Louise Germaine was born April 22, 1766. She remained an only child. Her mother took full charge of her upbringing and education, with the ambition of making her a model of intelligence and talent. She taught her English and Latin. Her program of reading and study was a severe one but was calculated to give Germaine wide interests and a strict Calvinist background. Unfortunately, Mme Necker never really cared for children, nor did she understand them, their need for play and especially for love. Consequently there was never a bond of deep affection between mother and daughter. In fact, there was conflict, which took the form of a sort of rivalry to be first in Jacques Necker's affections.

To the child Germaine, her father was everything she needed so desperately—friend, loving companion, and playmate. Her father loved her with spontaneous affection, which she returned to the degree of adoration. Germaine was naturally vivacious, gay, and frank. She impressed all by her remarkable intelligence and precocious questions. Her cousin, Mme Necker de Saussure, wrote, "She was always young, but never a child."[11]

In her early teens she read the novels of Richardson and Rousseau and the plays of Racine, in all of which love is the theme. Margaret Goldsmith wrote of Germaine's education: "She was carried into her mother's drawing room before she could walk. The social activities of her parents' homes were the background of her existence. The buzz of conversation was the first noise she could remember. Her mother's *salon* was Germaine's nursery."[12] "Her only childish trait was the making of paper kings and queens, and having them perform plays, usually tragedies. Perhaps her later habit of twisting a paper or green twig in her fingers as she talked stemmed from this early game."[13]

Soon after a visit to Geneva in 1767, Germaine's father was appointed minister of the Republic of Geneva to the court of Versailles. Two years later he became Director of the French India Company. These two appointments gave him power and social prestige, as well as *entrée* to the court of France.

The Neckers moved to a luxurious "hôtel" in the Rue de Cléry, and Mme Necker there began her famous "Fridays." Her *salon* was frequented by such notables of the "Philosophes" as Marmontel, Grimm, heavy and learned, the Abbés Raynal and Galiani, and the elderly Buffon, the naturalist. It was only after four years of ambitious effort that Suzanne succeeded in acquiring Diderot, impetuous and full of ideas, as one of her faithful. This group of intelligent, irreligious freethinkers, so foreign to Mme Necker's strict moral and religious orthodoxy, served as a publicity agency for her advancement of Necker. Even Voltaire yielded to her strategy and sang her praises, for it was she who was the prime mover in promoting the plan for a statue of Voltaire by Pigalle. The group that frequented Mme Necker's "Fridays" was a very powerful group of intellectuals who had great influence on public opinion and the press.

Germaine's Childhood

The importance of all this for Germaine, the future Mme de Staël, was the fact that her mother placed her on a small stool by her side at these social gatherings. Germaine's large eyes fixed on the speakers, drinking in every word and gesture. At times the venerable guests would talk to her as to an adult, give her a compliment, a joke, or ask about her studies. She came to feel that such public attention from great men was normal. It excited her. She heard conversations far beyond what was normal for her age and was encouraged to join in them. Some of these clever men wrote couplets to her.[14] They even gave her flattering classical names, such as Aglaë and Zulma.

When Germaine was eleven she was given a playmate of her own age for the first time. This was Catherine Huber, the daughter of a Swiss girlhood friend of Mme Necker, who was now in Paris. The two girls formed a true and lasting friendship.

Every afternoon Catherine Huber came to the Contrôle Général (Necker had been appointed to the position in 1776) and remained until ten in the evening. The two girls did their lessons together, but their chief delight was to choose a play from the Neckers' library, learn the parts, and act them out in the evening. This love of acting and of drama lasted throughout Germaine's life. She loved the great tragedies of Racine and Voltaire. Many years later at the château of Coppet these classical plays were to be the means of intellectual and emotional entertainment during periods of great stress.

Gradually the conflict between Germaine's glittering social environment and her mother's Calvinist austerity, between her own emotional intensity and the intellectual activity around her, put too great a strain on her health. Overstimulated by what she read and by the plays she saw, she wept at the least excuse.[15] Dr. Tronchin recommended a complete rest in the country. Now the strictly managed education by her mother ceased.

The entire summer of 1779 Germaine spent at Saint-Ouen, the country residence of the Neckers near Paris. She recovered her health but never lost her hypersensitivity. Sometimes Necker brought his wife and a few friends, Buffon, Marmontel, and the Abbé Raynal to witness one of the girl's plays. Most often he came alone to relax and rest in her young company. That summer began Germaine's complete and lasting devotion to her father.

He gave her the love she needed, enjoyed her conversation, and praised her activities. He never reproved her, but basked in the sunshine of her gay and spontaneous wit. He encouraged her natural conversational powers rather than her writing. Between Germaine and her mother there was tension and even a feeling of rivalry. Suzanne felt left out of the close relationship between father and daughter, but she was incapable of relaxing and playing with Germaine as did her husband. Suzanne Necker often suffered nervous *crises*, which would send her to bed for several days with violent migraines.

Necker and the Turn of Events

Up to this point we have concentrated on Germaine's childhood. Great events, however, were in preparation for France, and they were to become a major part of Germaine's life in which her father was to play an important role. Madame Necker's *salon* had been the means of making her husband well-known in influential circles among which his reputation as a financier was well publicized before he retired from the banking business and turned to writing. In 1773 he published his *Eloge de Colbert*, which was crowned by the French Academy, most of whose members met regularly at Mme Necker's *salon*.

In 1774 Louis XV died, and his young successor, Louis XVI, who was barely twenty, appointed Maurepas as Prime Minister with a good ministerial team. Turgot, Minister of Marine, and later promoted to *Contrôleur Général*, was a capable man of long experience as *Intendant* in Limoges.[16] He hoped to improve the government's serious financial situation without a catastrophe. He advocated strict accounting, stern economy, and better management of collecting taxes and royal monopolies. In 1776 he proposed to the king's council six edicts, one of which was to abolish the hated *corvée* (forced labor in lieu of taxation); another was to suppress the privileges of the guilds and corporations. These measures roused against him a storm of anger from the queen and her favorites down to the guilds. His attempts to repair the damage done by his predecessors failed; when Maurepas and the king failed to support him and his reforms, he was dismissed.[17]

The Neckers made a trip to London in 1775, perhaps to win support from the English banks but certainly to gain prestige. He published an essay on the Corn Laws, attacking Turgot's free-trade policy. With a little intrigue at court he succeeded in being named Turgot's successor in October, 1776. Was he not a great financier who had already loaned the government money?

Necker's Ideas and Personality

Necker believed that order should be brought into the chaotic finances of the government, that France was prosperous and sound, and that what was needed was to restore confidence and abolish waste and abuse.[18] When he was successful in floating huge loans, his friends sang his praises. He began to enjoy his popularity.

Germaine, though only ten years old at this time (1776), sat in her mother's *salon* listening to the discussions and the arguments of the physiocrats, of the inviolability of property, of the laissez faire policy, and, most important of all, she heard the presentation of the English ideas on constitutional government. Necker was sincerely a liberal in his thinking;[19] his sympathies were with the people. He saw to the distribution of corn to the hungry hordes of Paris. He wrote:

When we see how they (laborers) labor, and yet go hungry, we cannot but ask whether the earth was indeed created for a small minority of privileged persons, invested with the right to shut out their fellow men with hedges and fences from the gifts of God. Yet all the new laws give further protection to the superfluity of the satiated against the needy, to the strong against the weak, instead of the other way round.[20]

He firmly believed that the necessary financial and social reforms could be carried out within the framework of the government, failing to realize that it took more than financial magic at this point to save the situation. He himself served without salary, and the people thought him a great patriot.[21]

What kind of man was Jacques Necker? Physically, he was a large man, with small eyes, a large chin, and a receding forehead. He gave the impression of profundity by his apparent silent absent-mindedness. His mind was not quick, but methodical. To many he seemed governed by vanity and the love of popular acclaim.

Albert Leon Guerard in his history of France wrote the following appraisal:

Necker was no wizard and not even a statesman. But he was an excellent man and a good banker. He applied the well-tried methods of the accounting house to the welter of state finances; in particular, he attempted to fund, that is, to reduce to intelligibility that vast and loose monster, the national debt. It is hard to tell whether his plain and cautious methods would have restored the treasury to health, for the American War broke out and upset every prevision. In 1781 he published his "Compte-Rendu" or balance sheet of the country. . . . It announced a surplus when Necker knew there was a deficit. But it brought some light, however imperfect, into the chaos of the *régime*.[22]

It was the first balance sheet ever presented to the people. Among other things it revealed the extravagances of the court. Necker's published *Compte-Rendu* followed by his *Justification* of it brought on a flurry of hostile criticism and the king's resentment. Two ministers threatened to resign if Necker remained as minister. It was at this ill-chosen moment that Necker asked for full membership in the Council of Ministers; as a result he was dismissed by the king. On May 19, 1781 the Neckers moved to their château at Saint-Ouen, not far from Paris. Letters bewailing his loss to the nation poured in from all classes of people, but Necker had to enjoy this popularity in exile.

CHAPTER 2

Germaine and Eric Magnus

U P to this point the author's concern has been chiefly with Germaine's parents and the events of Necker's rise to political power and influence. It is Germaine Necker herself, the precocious daughter, who now claims attention. She had grown up in the midst of the ideological arguments and discussions of her mother's *salon,* and in an atmosphere of worship of her father.[1] The fires of Germaine's girlhood worship were later fanned to adulation by the throng of his admirers the day of his dismissal and exile to his home in Saint-Ouen.

She was now fifteen and not only had read Montesquieu's *L'Esprit des Lois* but had also made intelligent marginal comments. Its ideas she had heard discussed along with those of the physiocrats by such men as Marmontel, Diderot, Grimm, and Abbé Raynal. She had read *Clarissa Harlowe* of Richardson, *Paul et Virginie* of Bernardin de St. Pierre, *La Nouvelle Héloïse* of Jean-Jacques Rousseau and *Werther* of Goethe. The elopement of Clarissa in Richardson's novel was a principal event of Germaine's childhood.

At the age of fifteen Germaine was no longer a little girl. It was time for her parents to consider marriage for her. As the wealthiest young heiress in France, and a Protestant, Germaine was an object of special interest. Negotiations in behalf of the Swedish attaché, Eric Magnus, Baron de Staël-Holstein, a young favorite in court society, began when Germaine was only thirteen. Madame la Comtesse de Boufflers of the court entourage and the Swedish Ambassador, Count Creutz, both spoke for him as a suitable prospect to Mme Necker. To Mme Necker, however, De Staël was a nobody, and Germaine was the daughter of Jacques Necker, finance minister of France, which placed her above the lot of common young women. Since the Neckers insisted on a Protestant man of note, a proper match was not easy to find.

In 1783, when Germaine was seventeen, William Pitt, the English prodigy, and former Chancellor of the Exchequer at twenty-three, was in Paris. To Mme Necker, Pitt presented the right solution. She contemplated the marriage of England's most promising young statesman and the daughter of Necker, "France's tutelary genius." What a union it would be—England's outstanding statesman with this brilliant daughter of a great French statesman! Besides, England was now at peace with France. Madame Necker was certain her plans would bless all concerned. Whether Pitt was ever approached on the subject is unlikely. Germaine put an end to the project by her stubborn refusal to consider it. She would never consent to live in England, away from France.

There were violent emotional scenes in the household; Suzanne Necker took to her bed with a serious illness and reproached her daughter from what she thought was her deathbed.[2] Suzanne sent accusing letters to Germaine. On this, her deathbed, she would forgive her only on condition that Germaine would devote herself to her father and God after her death. Naturally, young Germaine was frightened and could no longer oppose her parents' wishes. She realized that hers would be a marriage for money and that her romantic dream of love was ended, at least for the time being. This crisis brought anguish to both mother and daughter and created a lasting coolness between them.

As a result of Germaine's unhappy refusal to consider Pitt, she offered no opposition when the official choice fell finally on the Swedish attaché, Baron Eric Magnus de Staël-Holstein, although he was seventeen years Germaine's senior. The marriage negotiations lasted three more years and involved both the Swedish King, Gustavus III, and the French court, including the queen and the Countess de Boufflers.[3]

Necker made several conditions in the marriage contract, which finally boiled down to the following: De Staël was to be guaranteed the ambassadorship of Sweden to France; Mlle Necker was never to go to Sweden against her will. The marriage contract was to be approved and signed by Queen Marie Antoinette. Sweden, asking for Tobago Island in the West Indies, was to receive instead St. Barthelémy.[4]

Eric Magnus

Eric Magnus de Staël-Holstein was the eighth child of a cavalry captain in an impoverished branch of a noble house. He knew poverty and had struggled to rise in the social sphere. Handsome, clever, and ambitious, he gained favor in the Swedish court. The day Gustavus III became the absolute monarch of Sweden by overthrowing its Constitution he noticed the ardor of a young and handsome ensign of the guard and promptly made him a lieutenant in his army. On a two-year leave De Staël learned the ways of the world through travel and on his return was named chamberlain to the Swedish queen.

Bored at the Swedish court, he applied for leave in 1776 to serve in the Expeditionary Force of George III to the American Colonies. This permission was granted, but instead he went to Paris, as did many Swedes, who were popular at the French court. King Gustavus was amused at De Staël's excuse for remaining in Paris—that he could not obtain a fitting post in the British forces—and appointed him attaché to the Swedish Ambassador, Count Creutz. This appointment gave him *entrée* to the court. His dark eyes, blond hair, finely chiseled features, and good manners won him favor with the ladies of the court. His easy spending ingratiated him with the queen. His great weakness, a fault common in that day, was gambling; he was never out of debt and was often in desperate circumstances. Only a rich marriage could save him and this he was determined to have. For seven years he persevered in efforts to marry the heiress of the Necker millions. He was to receive as her dowry 650,000 francs[5] ("pounds tournois").

Germaine met De Staël at Saint-Ouen in July, 1785. She wrote of him in her diary: "He's a man perfectly *honnête*, incapable of doing or saying a *sottise*, but sterile and lifeless [*sans ressort*]."[6] When they danced she observed that he danced well, but his glances lacked spirit, and his hand in hers was like white marble. Much later in her Journal, she wrote: "I am sorry not to have joined my fate to that of a great man. It is a woman's only glory on earth, but could I resign myself to England? Who knows whether the great man [Pitt] would have had heart—above all, who knows whether I would have loved him?"[7] Germaine and Eric Magnus were married January 14, 1786, in the Lutheran chapel of the Swedish Embassy, rue du Bac, Paris. The queen, the Swedish Count Fersen and the princes of the blood signed the contract.

Germaine and Marriage

For the first two or three years the De Staël household seemed outwardly one of unity. Germaine, however, had been ill-prepared for marriage by her mother. By nature passionate and idealistic, she found that marriage did not conform to her romantic ideas of it. To her, love meant the accord of two minds, which seek to melt into an impossible embrace, and that is why physical beauty was only to her a complementary quality, which was not always the base of the torment that passion made her experience. She sought first the high intellectual joys of the marriage of minds.[8] De Staël fell far short of this ideal.

She captured her friends and lovers by an intuitive ability to please. Since she was not beautiful she renounced coquetry and guile and relied on frankness, an amazing and unlimited generosity, intellectual brilliance, and her passionate enthusiasm.

She expressed in her writings her belief that marriage is the firm basis of a civilized society. Her ideal was a lasting affection and she sought it unsuccessfully the rest of her life. This search for happiness in love was the basis of her change of lovers. The only true and lasting affection she found in her turbulent life was with a handsome, dashing French officer of twenty-three, who met her and fell in love with her when she was forty-five, six years before her death!

Shortly after her marriage to De Staël she was presented at court. The story of her awkwardness—how she stepped on her skirt trimmings, tore them, and was assisted to their repair through the kindness of the queen—she repeated about herself good-naturedly.[9] It is an example of her straightforward frankness. The ladies of the court, however, smiled with malice. Those who hated Necker indulged their spleen upon his daughter. She was criticized for her witty talk, for her sometimes tactless remarks and questions, and for her frank disregard of social conventions. Her chief fault was her consciousness of her intellectual superiority.

As Ambassadress she wrote to King Gustavus regular bulletins of court news.

The Queen's balls are very splendid. The hall is arranged as a fairy palace. The gardens of the Trianon are there, and fountains of water play continually; pastoral ideas, reveries that the country inspires, mingled with the splendors of the luxury of the courts. In another hall you witness recreations but little [that is] pastoral—reckless gambling. Young M. Castellane has had to quit his paternal home for having lost here in one evening the whole of his fortune. The Queen sets an example of moderation; and it is not on her account that her court is ruining itself. But the gamesters tire of every other occupation. They find everything else insipid. They have acquired the taste for great excitements . . .[10]

However, court etiquette and amusements did not appeal to her for long. She found the conversation trivial and frivolous. Her own *salon* in the rue du Bac held the intellectual excitement she enjoyed, the flashing interchange of ideas and of witty epigrams among the best minds of her time, including politicians, scientists, and men of letters.

With her title of Ambassadress, Germaine felt herself emancipated after her marriage. She received large numbers of guests at the Swedish embassy and entertained elaborately. Her overflowing vitality and her superior mind were well expressed by her vigorous, outgoing nature. Many people were at first repelled by her personality. Madame de Boufflers, the good friend of de Staël, wrote Gustavus III about Germaine:

She is imperious and strong-willed to excess, and she has a self-assurance that I have never seen matched by any person of her age, no matter of what rank.[11]

Gouverneur Morris, representative of the new American government at the French court, was often a guest in her *salon*. He wrote:

In the midst of her guests stood the hostess, in her favorite attitude before the fire, with her hands behind her back, a large leonine woman, with few beauties and no grace of gesture. She nevertheless animated the salon by her masculine attitude and powerful conversation.[12]

Madame de Staël later became a life-long friend of his.

Germaine de Staël was never beautiful. She was of average height, somewhat stocky, with an uneven complexion and full lips. She wore her black hair long and curling, in later years in ringlets framed by a turban. One of the most flattering portraits of her, painted by Mme Vigée-Lebrun, displays a jewelled turban. She was proud of her shoulders and arms, which she customarily left bare. Her greatest asset was her large, dark, and and unusually expressive eyes. Albert Sorel describes her:

A strong nose, a mouth forcibly designed, prominent lips opening wide for life and speech, the mouth of an orator, with a frank and kindly smile; all her genius shines forth in her eyes, in her sparkling glances, confiding, superb, deep and sweet when in repose, imperious when lighted by a sudden flash. . . . Germaine must speak in order to charm, and must conquer in order to make herself beloved . . .[13]

On July 31, 1787, Germaine's baby girl was born. She was christened Edwige-Gustavine, after her godfather, Gustavus III. A thin, weak baby, she lived only twenty months. During this period many tremendous currents of change were eddying under the apparently calm surface of aristocratic French society. Necker's recall to the ministry became imminent as the Assembly of Notables refused to pass the social reforms which had now become imperious, reforms which Turgot had sponsored in the day when they might have averted revolution.

Germaine's First Works

Madame de Staël's first works were romantic love stories, some probably written before, and some soon after, her marriage. They were not published until later, probably in 1795. Her father affectionately called her "Monsieur Saint-Ecritoire" and prevented her from publishing. At the age of nineteen she wrote in her Journal:

My father is quite right. Women are not meant to choose the same path as men; why compete with them? Why excite a jealousy in them which would differ so much from that excited by love? A woman should call nothing her own, and she should only find happiness in that of the man she loves.[14]

Her ideas were changed by destiny. She did not find happiness in that of the man she married, nor in that of the men she loved. The path she chose to follow in her political activity after her marriage was more that of a man than that of a woman, but a woman in those days had no political rights. She never published anything under her maiden name. *Sophie, ou les Sentiments Secrets* and *Jane Gray*, dramas in verse, were written about 1786-87. Other early works were short "Nouvelles," *Mirza, Adélaïde et Théodore*, and *Pauline*. They were all essays of her youth, stories of unhappy tragic lovers described by Sainte-Beuve as "enveloped in sensitivity as by a cloud, lovers who fade away and die as they learn of infidelity."[15] They treat of marriage and tragic love. *Pauline* presents a case of injustice to all women, *Mirza* of injustice to a woman of intelligence and genius who errs in passion, is abandoned, and commits suicide. The story foreshadows the tormenting problem of Mme de Staël's life.[16] Its plot is set in exotic Senegal. Germaine had been influenced by her reading, but she was not interested in nature nor in the exotic as such. She portrayed her own purpose, which was the declaration of her own ideas on love and on the status of women.

Adélaïde et Théodore can be called, in the words of the critic Larg, "A nascent novel of manners, with a perfect picture of the man of the *ancien régime*."[17] She already shows her dislike of the cynicism of men of the world, of the brainless frivolity of their women, and of the hidden malice beneath their polished manners.

Letters on Jean-Jacques Rousseau

Germaine's first work of literary importance was *Letters on the Writings and Character of Jean-Jacques Rousseau*. Written when she was twenty-two and first printed for private circulation, it showed not only her early admiration for the author of *Julie, ou la Nouvelle Héloïse*, but also her debt to him. Sainte-Beuve called it a hymn nourished with serious thoughts varied with acute observations.[18]

The *Letters* were a success; for a girl of twenty-two they were a brilliant work. They show her enthusiastic ideals and reaction against the frivolous negation around her. She agrees with Rousseau that only ecstasy leads to eternal truths. She defines genius as "the particular alliance of thought and emotion"; in other words, reason illuminated for flight by deep passionate emotion.[19] The eloquence of Rousseau calls forth her deep admiration. She discusses the moral questions in *Julie;* Julie's remorse, resignation, and the conduct of the rest of her life make the book moral. Julie's fault is not through excess of passion and is therefore greater than if it were.

In "Letter III" she discusses *Emile.* She approves of his inspiring mothers to care for their children themselves, for a mother's love is equally important for mother and child. Servants make the children into little tyrants. She can adopt some details of his system of education, but she rejects it on the whole as impractical. For her own son she would prefer an education for a career. Rousseau's eloquence is such that at each page she says "yes," but at the end of the book she says "surely it is false."

She disagrees with his education of a woman as a dependent and inferior being. By painting Sophie as betraying her husband, Rousseau condemns his whole system of education. She ends her letter with an adoring eulogy of her father for his work, *The Importance of Religious Opinions.*

"Letter IV" deals with Rousseau's discussion of the constitution of governments, the most important subject of that tim' *The Social Contract* of Rousseau establishes the true foundations of all legitimate power; namely, no government should be established without the consent of the governed. Germaine reproaches Rousseau for not judging a nation free that has its representatives as legislators, and for insisting, instead, on the general assembly of all individuals. She contrasts the work of Montesquieu with that of Jean-Jacques and prefers the former because it is not speculative but is founded on the observation of facts; it is practical. She counsels her readers to beware of exaggeration, and her prayer is that the coming assembly of national representatives be guided by reason.

"Letter V" discusses Rousseau's works on music and botany. His musical romances are simple, melancholy, and touching. The sixth and last "Letter" is perhaps the most interesting. It describes Rousseau's character and shows unusual power of analysis. She believes Rousseau is sincerely picturing himself in his *Confessions.* It is his thought in solitude which makes him impassioned—"He dreamed rather than existed." Imagination was his greatest faculty and sometimes it destroyed his affections and friendships.

The following eloquent passage displays her own thought and her sympathy for Jean-Jacques. "To be two in the world calms so many fears! The judgments of men, and even of God, seem less to be feared. One makes so small an empty space in one's own eyes, when one does not occupy a place in another's heart who survives us, that it is possible to count one's life for naught."[20] She abhorred the solitude that Rousseau extolled.

Rousseau was not insane; he was "en démence." He had great power of reason, which he displayed on abstract subjects but not at all in practical matters. Paris upset him, for he was born for the quiet, contemplative life in nature which he described so eloquently. He hated society and its institutions and finally succumbed to his feelings of persecution, to his morbid suspicions that he was hated by everyone. Unable to bear it any longer, he took his own life. (Many critics, however, have not accepted her belief that he committed suicide.)

It has been said that through her study of Rousseau she revealed her own soul. She wrote: "Many celebrated writers have put the germ of all their future works in their first work. In youth thought is a tumultuous affair. We probably have within us all the ideas we shall ever have, but it is still chaos within us. [Later they come] under the yoke of reason."

Germaine's ideas expressed in the *Letters* were certainly within her but not in chaos. The following ideas remained true in her later work. "A novel can be a painting of the customs or absurdities of the moment or a play of imagination which unites extraordinary events to captivate the interest or curiosity, or (it may be) a great moral idea put into action and rendered dramatic."[21] The virtue of men is in combating passion and that of women is in triumphing over it. Both *Julie* and *Delphine* are examples of this struggle. Contrary to Rousseau, and she reproached him for his doing so, she did not seek the Golden Age in the past but in man's progressive development.

CHAPTER 3

The Revolution Begins

AFTER Necker's first dismissal from the Ministry in May, 1781, the family retired to Saint-Ouen. His published justification of his *Compte-Rendu* sold eighty thousand copies. In it he showed that twenty-five million francs yearly were wasted on useless pensions and gratifications, in particular to the Polignac family, friends of the queen; that collectors got one-fifth of the revenues; and that nearly all the national institutions of charity and penal reform were mismanaged.[1] This publication provoked the king, had the effect of a bombshell on the nation, and was the cause of Necker's dismissal. He retired to Saint-Ouen, from which point he could watch with agony of soul the menacing steps toward the dissolution of the king's power. During the first days of Necker's retirement, however, he was the object of praise and sympathy. Germaine wrote at Saint-Ouen, "Everybody came to see him; noblemen, clergy, magistrates, merchants, men of letters, all flocked to Saint-Ouen. More than 500 letters, received from members of the provincial boards and corporations, expressed a degree of respect and affection, which had, perhaps, never been shown to a public man in France."[2]

It was during this period at Saint-Ouen that Germaine's affection for her father became a strong and steady passion in her life. After his death it was a deep worship which she revealed in her writings on the French Revolution.

Château at Coppet

In 1784 Necker bought the beautiful old château of Coppet on Lake Geneva. Here he was to spend much time for the next seven years before his final tragic recall to the ministry. It was a refuge for Mme Necker, whose health was threatened by periodic nervous crises. To Germaine it was a painful exile from the Paris she loved and craved. She hated its "infernal quiet."

The château was situated on a slight elevation near Lake Geneva. It opened on a court flanked by two wings and faced the park with flowering shrubs, stately trees, and graveled walks. From the windows of the second story the view extended over the red-tiled roofs of the town, over the dazzling blue of the lake, to the snow-capped peaks of the Alps in the distance. Coppet was to become Mme de Staël's home in exile.

Failure of the Ministers to Solve France's Problems

During the years of Necker's retirement one minister followed another in the attempt to keep the king's ship of state afloat. Their policies, however, were those of blind reaction, while the people protested ever more loudly against the feudal rights so obviously obsolete. In 1783, the Minister Colonne tried for four years the policy of prodigal spending, which delighted the courtiers. Seeing the day of reckoning approaching, he decided to put into action Turgot's reforms and Necker's orthodox financing.[3] The reactionaries called for his dismissal, and Loménie de Brienne, Archbishop of Toulouse, took over the task of Finance Minister, calling upon the Assembly of Notables to back him. They, however, refused and brought up the subject of calling the States General. These had not been convened for one hundred and seventy years; the last occasion had been in 1614. Brienne now tried governing by edicts instead, but the Parliament of Paris, which had to register the edicts, refused to cooperate and also called for the convening of the States General.

The feeling of the people was becoming more and more hostile to the privileged classes. In 1784 Beaumarchais's *The Marriage of Figaro* was performed against the king's wishes.[4] It ridiculed the society of the *ancien régime* without mercy and applauded the rise to importance of a member of the lower class. On top of this came the scandal of the Diamond Necklace, which falsely involved the queen and aroused violent feeling against her.[5]

The true story[6] of this scandal was that of a court intrigue involving the ambitious Cardinal de Rohan and a crystal-ball-reading adventuress, Mme de la Motte who claimed she could influence the queen to have him appointed to the ministry. For this he should purchase a necklace of great price in the name

of and for the queen, and at a certain jeweller's in Paris. The
naïve cardinal did so and gave the necklace to Mme de la Motte,
who promptly sold the jewels. When the jeweller came to Marie
Antoinette for payment, the whole affair was publicly aired and
judgment was made by the Parlement de Paris, but the damage
to the Queen's reputation had been done and she was more hated
than ever. Many people did not believe in the Queen's innocence.
Even in 1793, at the revolutionary trial of Marie Antoinette, she
was again falsely accused of these charges.

Finally in August, 1788, the bewildered King recalled Jacques
Necker to power. When Germaine, enthusiastic and happy,
brought the news of his recall to her father, Necker was heavy-
hearted, for he felt that it was too late. "Ah, why did they
not give me those fifteen months of the Archbishop of Lens
[Brienne]?"[7]

Events followed quickly. The States General was convened
May 3, 1789. Necker persuaded the king to double the Third
Estate, making it equal to the other two estates, the Nobles and
the Clergy.[8] It was a revolutionary move, but a necessary one if
any system of reform were to pass. The crucial question now
concerned the method of voting. This was left to be decided
later on. On the one hand, the aristocracy of birth and of the
church, and on the other, the liberals, were adamant in their
opposing demands. The king was caught between them.

Already the provinces were aroused, taxes were virtually un-
collected, and the government was facing bankruptcy. The hard
winter of 1788, the coldest in eighty years, and the ensuing bad
harvests caused incredible misery. Jobless workers crowded into
Paris by the thousands to obtain bread. Necker personally fi-
nanced the purchase of wheat to feed the starving Paris populace.[9]

Political Pamphlets and Discussions

The nation, and especially Paris, was flooded with pamphlets
proposing reforms and ideas for constitutional government. Discussions were held not only in the *salons* but in the cafés and
on the street corners. New flames of hope were being lighted in
the hearts of the people, that heavy and unjust burdens would
be lifted from their shoulders. This new hope was to become an
inextinguishable fire, burning for liberty and equality.

During the elections to the States General of 1789 the people were provided with excellent training in politics. Here was a chance to air their grievances. The liberal thinkers and writers with no practical experience held forth daily about the rights of the governed, about the relation of men to one another and to government. Jean-Jacques Rousseau's ideas from the *Social Contract* were widely known. Men believed they could establish a new and simple system for the complex and traditional order of the day. They did not see the dangers in such a sudden uprooting of the long-established basis of law and custom before the new order of justice had been established.[10]

"To comprehend the contrast between the benign theories and the violent acts of the Revolution, one must remember that it was prepared by the most civilized classes of the nation, and executed by the roughest and most unpolished."[11] This last class was hardened by suffering and was as ready to inflict suffering as to bear it.

Neither Mme de Staël nor her father completely realized the impossibility of compromise and moderation which was developing, not only in Paris, but throughout France. Equality was the great watchword, but liberty was the cry of all the reformers from La Fayette to Camille Desmoulins.

When Necker was recalled to the Ministry in 1788, his chief work during that bitter winter and spring was to keep the people of Paris from starving and to keep the bankrupt government going. He deposited two million francs from his own pocket in the Treasury.

The States General

At last the great days, May 4 and May 5, arrived. The States General, twelve hundred strong, assembled in Versailles. Madame de Staël watched the imposing procession from a window. She wrote:

I shall never forget the hour that I saw the twelve hundred deputies of France pass in procession to Church to hear Mass, the day before the opening of the Assembly. It was a very imposing sight, and very new to the French; all the inhabitants of Versailles, and many persons attracted by curiosity from Paris, collected to see it. This new kind

of authority in the state, of which neither the nature nor the strength
was as yet known, astonished the greater part of those who had not
reflected on the rights of nations. . . . [the Tiers Etat] their imposing numbers, their confident looks, their black coats and dresses, fixed
the attention of the spectators. Literary men, merchants, and a great
number of lawyers, formed the chief part of this order.[12]

Mirabeau, the aristocrat, was one of the Third Estate. She
describes him:

The eye that was once fixed on his countenance was not likely to be
soon withdrawn. His immense head of hair distinguished him from
amongst the rest, and suggested the idea that, like Samson, his
strength depended on it; his countenance derived expression even
from its ugliness; and his whole person conveyed the idea of irregular
power, but still such power as we should expect to find in a tribune
of the people . . . I confess I gave myself up to the liveliest hope
on seeing national representatives for the first time in France. Madame
de Montmorin [wife of the Minister of Foreign Affairs] said to me . . .
in a way which made an impression upon me, "You do wrong to
rejoice; this will be the source of great misfortunes to France and
to us."[13]

Necker's speech before the States General contained many
facts showing improved finances and taxation but nothing about
the constitutional changes expected by the Assembly. It lasted
three hours. After thirty minutes Necker's voice became hoarse,
and it was a clerk who finished the reading. The speech was a
disappointment to the deputies who had expected so much. It
dealt at length and with dry statistics on the public debt and
taxation, but it did not mention the fact that the treasury was
empty.

On May 5 the States General were convened in the great hall
created in the avenue of Versailles to receive the deputies.
Madame de Staël wrote: "When the King came to seat himself on
his throne in the midst of this assembly, I felt, for the first time,
a sensation of fear. I observed that the Queen was much agitated;
she came after the appointed time, and her color was visibly
altered."[14] Madame de Staël's anxiety came from the contrast
of the King's unemphatic dry manner of speaking with the
energetic, aroused look of the deputies. There was need for a
balance of force and the King showed none of this.

For five weeks the various bodies discussed the questions of voting, whether by head or by order, and the renunciation by the upper orders of the tax-exemption privilege. Precious time was lost; tempers rose. Finally, on June 17 the Third Estate passed a decree declaring itself the "National Assembly of France" and inviting the other orders to join it. Here was the beginning of the Revolution, according to Mme de Staël.[15] Liberal (en-lightened) members of the other two orders, the nobility and the clergy, accepted the invitation of the "Tiers." Its influence grew apace.

In her assessment of the first two months of the sessions of the States General, Mme de Staël speaks of the idealism of the great number of intelligent and philosophic minds in France in 1789. She continues with an analysis of the defeat of the moderates. "Yet the ignorance of the people in Paris, and still more in the country, that ignorance which results from the long oppression and neglected education of the lower orders, contained the seeds of all those misfortunes which afterwards overpowered France. Of distinguished men, the country contained perhaps as many as England; but the stock of good sense that belongs to a free nation did not exist in France. Religion founded on inquiry, education generally diffused, the liberty of the press, and the right of voting at public elections, are sources of improvement which had been in operation in England for more than a century."[16]

This was the need in France, and the desire of the Third Estate was to bring about this new *régime*. Long discussions, however, wearied the Assembly, and factions arose which relied on the taking of energetic measures. When the Third Estate felt itself threatened by the rumor of advancing troops, and by being shut out from its place of assembly by preparations for the royal sitting, it met on the Tennis Court, and "bound themselves by an oath to maintain the national rights."[17]

Declaration of Rights

La Fayette read his "Declaration of the Rights of Man" on July 11. "Every man is born with inalienable and unprescribable rights; these are: the freedom of his opinions, the care for honour and his life, the right of property, the entire disposition of his person, the products of his industry and all his faculties, the communication of his thoughts by every possible means, the pursuit of happiness, and the resistance of oppression."[18]

Of this "Declaration of Rights," Mme de Staël wrote in *Considerations*: "On the 11th July, before the Tiers Etat had obtained their triumphs, M. de la Fayette addressed the Constituent Assembly, and proposed a Declaration of Rights similar to that which the Americans placed at the head of their constitution, after declaring their independence. The English, likewise, after excluding the Stuarts and calling William III to the crown, made him sign a Bill of Rights, on which their present constitution is founded."[19]

She felt that the French declaration should have been confined to indisputable facts and should have left out matters capable of "dangerous interpretation." "There can be no doubt that distinctions in society can have no other object than the general good; that all political power takes its rise from the interest of the people; that men are born and remain free and equal in the eye of the law; but there is ample space for sophistry in so wide a field, while nothing is more clear or undoubted than the application of these truths to individual liberty, the establishment of juries, the freedom of the press, popular elections, the division of the legislative power, the sanctioning of taxes," etc.[20] She saw the danger of the argumentative discussion which followed in the succeeding months.

The National Assembly remained busy with its project of formulating a constitution. In Paris groups were meeting everywhere for discussion, but especially in the gardens of the Palais Royal belonging to the Duke of Orléans. Leaders like Camille Desmoulins climbed on tables and orated on the dangers facing the country. "The newspapers published the debates of the Assembly. The press was exciting the public mind."[21]

On June 23 came the Royal Sitting. Necker disapproved of it and was conspicuously absent. The King ordered the Assembly to sit in their separate houses. The Third Estate alone refused to follow him out. When the Grand Master of Ceremonies ordered them out, Mirabeau, the people's orator, hurled his defiance: "Tell your master we are here by the will of the people, and shall not leave except under the force of bayonets."[22]

Louis yielded, sending word to the privileged orders to join the Third Estate. This vacillation of the King made Necker's position impossible. His hope of a middle course between the royalists and the revolutionists was dashed forever when the King now secretly sought the help of troops. Madame de Staël described the situation in *Considerations on the Principal Events of the French Revolution.*

"My father told us in confidence every evening that he expected to be put under arrest next day; but that the danger to which the King was exposed, was, in his opinion, so great that he deemed it his duty to remain in office, that he might not appear to suspect what was going on."[23]

On July 11, Necker, while at dinner, received his dismissal, which he was ordered to keep secret. After dinner he told his wife about it in confidence, then wrote a few notes, including one to Germaine, who had left for Paris. He called for his carriage as if going for an afternoon's drive, and he and Suzanne set out for Brussels, the nearest frontier. Germaine received her father's note the next day, but the news was already public. With M. de Staël beside her she arrived after an exhausting journey at Necker's hotel in Brussels.

Sunday, July 12, the news of Necker's dismissal caused thousands to flock to the Palais Royal. There Camille Desmoulins stood on a table and, flourishing a pistol, he shouted, "Citizens, there is no time to lose; the dismissal of Necker is the knell of Saint Bartholomew for patriots. This very night all the Swiss and German battalions will leave the Champs de Mars to massacre us all; one resource is left: to take arms."[24]

Leaves were torn from the trees to be worn as the green of the Necker livery. The busts of Necker and the Duke of Orléans were paraded. When the mob met opposition from the dragoons of the Prince de Lambesc, blood flowed.

The Fall of the Bastille

False rumors flew that the guns of the Bastille were pointed on the Rue Saint Antoine, the most populous quarter of Paris. The crowds gathered. Great fears were aroused, for the Bastille had become the symbol of oppression and royal authority. With its fall the revolution was begun in earnest. There was a parley with the governor of the Bastille, De Launay, but the crowds became impatient, broke loose, and tore off the chains of the drawbridge to the prison. They rushed in and for four hours the fight raged. De Launay and other defenders were massacred.[25]

The King was forced to recall Necker from Switzerland. Germaine describes the trip back to Paris. "The transports of the people, my father's carriage drawn by the citizens of the towns through which we passed . . . women on their knees when they saw him pass along the road."[26]

The day after his arrival Necker presented himself at the Hôtel de Ville. Madame de Staël gives a full description of the scene and of her emotions on that wonderful day:

The last of pure happiness in my life. The whole population of Paris rushed in crowds into the streets; men and women were seen at the windows, and on the roofs calling out, "Vive M. Necker." As he drew near the Hôtel de Ville the acclamations redoubled, the square was filled with a multitude animated by one feeling, and pressing forward to receive a single man, and that man was my father. Hardly had M. Necker pronounced the word amnesty, than it came home to every heart; the people collected in the square were eager to participate in it. M. Necker then came forward on the balcony, and proclaiming in a loud voice the sacred words of peace among Frenchmen of all parties, the whole multitude answered him with transport. As for me I saw nothing after this instant, for I was bereft of my senses by joy.[27]

The March on Versailles

Necker's speech at the Hôtel de Ville declared an amnesty and asked for the release of the Baron de Busenval, commander of the troops around Paris, who had been arrested by the revolutionaries as hostile to them. This act of Necker's was hardly a measure to solidify his popularity with the people, and gradually he proved himself not the strong man needed to save the situation. He and Mirabeau, the people's orator in the Assembly, did not see eye to eye.

The court intrigues were too strong, and the King showed a fatal indecision. In the National Assembly, however, the work on the Constitution went steadily along. On August 4, 1789, the

Assembly, swept by the wind of enthusiastic idealism, decreed the abolition of privileges and feudal rights in France. Guerard calls this, "An unprecedented triumph of generosity and reason."[28] It was an example of the idealistic enthusiasm of the liberals ruling the Assembly, the friends and acquaintances of Mme de Staël.

It was in her *salon* that the constitutionalists both of the right and the left met and discussed the reforms. These men included not only her closest friends, Louis de Narbonne, Talleyrand, and Mathieu de Montmorency but also Siéyès, Brissot, Condorcet of the left, and Malouet, François de Jaucourt, Lally Tollendal, Barnave, and the Lameths of the right. It was under the tutelage of her brilliant and vital personality that the constitutional ideas were discussed and formulated. Influenced by Montesquieu, she was at this time an advocate of a constitutional monarchy on the order of that in England. Only later, in 1793, when she saw the impossibility of a constitutional monarchy, did she favor a republic. On August 27 came the vote in the Assembly on the "Declaration of the Rights of Man," modeled on the American declaration.[29]

On this early period of the National Assembly and its enthusiasms, Mme de Staël commented:

The Assembly was seized with a philosophic enthusiasm, proceeding in part from the example of the United States of America. . . . The French flattered themselves with the power of adopting for the basis of their government the principles which suited a new people; but, situated in the midst of Europe, and embarrassed with a privileged caste, whose claims it was necessary to quiet, the plan was impracticable: besides, how were they to conciliate the institutions of a republic with the existence of a monarchy? The English Constitution offered the only example of the solution of this problem. But a mania, something like that of a man of letters, prompted the French to innovate in this respect. . . . When real institutions are in question, we are fortunate in having before us a practical proof of their utility.[30] [She meant the English government.]

Rumor the King Would Leave: Reaction in Paris

On the part of the court and its royalist factions, however, there was still plotting for the use of troops. The Queen appeared amidst great applause at a banquet of loyalist officers. This alarmed the people that troops might be used against them. Early in October came the rumor that the King would attempt to leave the country. The women of the central market, Les Halles, in Paris took the offensive against the court. The well-known extravagance of the ladies of the court while the common people were suffering aroused them to action. On October 5 the mob marched the twelve miles from Paris to Versailles, armed with whatever it could lay its hands on and increasing as it went. Their belief was that the return of their king to Paris would somehow release them from misery. La Fayette and his National Guards followed the crowd and held it in check the next day.

Madame de Staël tells the story of those two tragic days:

I was apprised on the morning of the 5th of October that the populace was marching to Versailles; my mother and father had their residence there. . . . M. Necker proceeded very quickly to the palace, to be present at the council; and my mother, more and more frightened by the threatening intelligence received from Paris, repaired to the hall which served as an antechamber to the council room, that she might share my father's fate, whatever it might be. I followed her . . .

The King decided on awaiting the Parisian army, or rather multitude, which had already begun its march; and every eye was turned towards the road that fronts the windows of the palace at Versailles. . . . We were informed of the arrival of M. de La Fayette at the head of the National Guards. At last M. de La Fayette entered the palace and crossed the hall where we were, to go to the King . . . to assure the safety of the palace he desired to occupy the posts of the interior; the exterior posts only were given to him. . . . We all went home after midnight thinking that the crisis of the day was over . . .

On the 6th of October at a very early hour, a lady . . . came in panic to seek refuge among us. . . . She informed me that assassins had made their way even to the Queen's antechamber, that they had massacred several of her guards at the door, and that awakened by their cries, the Queen had saved her life only by fleeing into the King's room by a private passage.

The people demanded with great clamor that the King and royal family should remove to Paris; an answer in assent had been given on their part, and the cries and the firing which we heard were signs of rejoicing from the Parisian troops. The Queen then appeared in the hall, her hair dishevelled, her countenance pale but dignified. . . .

The Queen advanced without hesitation along with her two children, who served as bodyguard . . . to the balcony. There La Fayette bent and kissed her hand.

The multitude seemed affected at seeing the Queen as a mother, and political rage became appeased at the sight; those who that very night had perhaps wished to assassinate her extolled her name to the skies.[31]

King and Queen Established in the Tuileries

The King and Queen were taken to Paris with the heads of their slain bodyguards on the points of pikes. The King's authority was now at an end, and he and his family were established in the Tuileries in the care of "his good people of Paris." They were virtually prisoners. Louis acknowledged secretly to Spain that henceforth no act or word of his would express his own will.[32]

The following year on July 14, 1790, at the great "Festival of the Celebration" at the Champs de Mars, Louis appeared at the Festival's Altar of the Fatherland and swore allegiance to the still unfinished constitution. This great day of enthusiasm for, and love of, the King was followed by intrigue and the emigration of many nobles.

Of this abandonment of country Mme de Staël wrote in *Considerations* that the first principle of patriotism is never to hand over one's country to foreigners for any reason, however good the cause.[33] She felt that had the *émigrés* remained to help the situation in the early part of the Revolution, the course of history might have been changed. Their departure opened the way to the democratic crisis in which passionate men were carried away by the tidal wave called equality.[34]

Necker, who disagreed with many of the radical reforms of the Assembly, resorted to memorials to give his advice. He grew thin and was sometimes rude and overbearing as he saw his influence of no avail. Neither he nor Germaine, living in wealth and security, were able to realize the strength of the political forces that were now building up in men like Desmoulins, Danton, and Marat. Finally, seeing that his efforts to save the monarchy were futile, he resigned.

After Necker's resignation and retirement to Coppet in September, 1790, Germaine remained in Paris and gave birth to

Gustave on August 25.[35] In October she followed her parents to Coppet where she remained for eleven months. She left behind her all that she loved, her *salon*, her friends, and her lover. She hoped to comfort her father who was miserable in his sense of failure.

CHAPTER 4

Narbonne

IT WAS IN 1788 that she had fallen deeply, passionately, in love with Count Louis de Narbonne. He was thirty-three; she was twenty-two. He was handsome, intelligent, sensitive, and selfish and a notorious conqueror of feminine hearts. He possessed an indefinable charm of manner and a dash of idealism.

Madame de Staël's marriage of convenience had not fulfilled her romantic dreams. She and de Staël were temperamentally incompatible. She hated his gambling and was not very tolerant of his lack of intellectual gifts. During the early years of their marriage, their union became chiefly a friendly business arrangement the purpose of which, from her point of view, was to further her father's career. Each was free to live his own life. Her concept of love required "an intellectual and nervous exaltation."[1] Beside the brilliant wit of a Talleyrand, the charm of a Narbonne, or the gentle idealism of a Mathieu de Montmorency, her husband was a disappointment to her. Her exuberant nature was capable of both loyal friendship and passionate love. She served her friends at the peril of her life during the Terror, but she dominated and possessed them. Her great fault was her restless, unsatisfied temperament, which sought fulfillment in more than one love relationship, sometimes more than one at a time.

Narbonne

Narbonne had been brought up at court as a prince of the blood royal. Mystery surrounded his parentage. He ran through three fortunes and commanded a regiment without ever having served in it.[2] In the royal armies only noblemen could serve as officers. Narbonne was altogether a dashing gentleman with superior social charm and conversational wit. Germaine was madly in love with him and did not conceal it. The Revolution and exile bound them together, but for Narbonne the episode with Germaine was only one of many.

Germaine was attracted to two other aristocrats of birth and breeding, Talleyrand, about whom she had no illusions, and Mathieu de Montmorency. Talleyrand she put into her novel *Delphine,* as the treacherous, scheming Mme de Vernon. Mathieu was a gentle friend and aristocrat and was loyal to her all his life. It was Talleyrand's mind that stimulated her. She is said to have helped him with his famous report on Public Instruction in 1790. Her friendship for Mathieu was of a different origin. Grieving for his loss of a beloved cousin, he needed her to console him. Later on it was his ever loyal friendship, which protected and comforted her in her troubled life.

Madame de Staël's Purpose for Narbonne

The passion that preoccupied her life for at least six years, however, was Louis de Narbonne. With him she would reform the world, eliminate the abuses of the *ancien régime,* conduct the Revolution to a successful constitutional monarchy, and create a society founded on progress and the goal of the perfectibility of man.[3] In her *salon* she assembled most of the men of influence and talent for her political dream but the confusion of opposing minds at court, in the Assembly, and among the people brought to nought any such moderate accomplishment.

She did manage to have Narbonne appointed Minister of War. In three months, in a whirlwind of activity, he reorganized the army and the frontier defenses. However, the King did not trust him and dismissed him from office. Narbonne joined La Fayette and his army and received a mission to Paris.

Gouverneur Morris, who sympathized with the aristocrats, wrote to President Washington on November 22, 1790:

This unhappy country, bewildered in the pursuit of metaphysical whimsies, presents to our moral view a mighty ruin. The sovereign humbled to the level of a beggar's pity, without resources, without authority, without a friend. The Assembly at once a master and a slave, new in power, wild in theory, raw in practice. It engrosses all functions though incapable of exercising any, and has taken from this fierce and ferocious people every restraint of religion and respect. One thing only seems to be tolerably ascertained, that the opportunity is lost and (for the time at least) the Revolution has failed.[4]

Mme de Staël was far from agreeing with him. Full of youthful hope and confidence, she felt success was still possible. She delighted in the struggle; she was convinced of its ultimate success. She felt that the salvation of France lay in the hands of select, intelligent, enlightened minds, and she labored to bring them together in her *salon* for free discussion. She was the life and soul of these discussions in her superior intelligence, enthusiasm, and wit. Conversation was her element, and through it she fired the imagination and sparked the motives of those around her.

The year 1791 saw the unsuccessful attempt in June of the King to flee from France, which ended in his arrest at Varennes, and his return to Paris. From then on Mme de Staël's efforts toward the formation of a constitutional monarchy seemed doomed to failure. She was lambasted by both the right and the left but remained unmoved, unswerving in her liberal ideas. She worked for the establishment of the Constitution of Siéyès and La Fayette, which, above all, guaranteed liberty and which she thought would be capable of correcting whatever defects it might prove to have in the eyes of both right and left. These "defects" were the controversial articles concerning the status of the Church, the veto, and the method of financing the government. Mme de Staël knew that the Royalist forces of the right would lead back to absolutism and the forces of the left to mob rule. She saw the necessity for conciliation of the two sides, and she pleaded and worked for moderation.

In September, 1791, the Constituent Assembly ended its work. With tragic results it passed Robespierre's motion that none of the former members could be re-elected to the Legislative Assembly that met October 1. Thus, none of the experienced members could serve. The Revolution, now deprived of its guiding moderate authors, began all over again, with the conservatives and the radicals in bloody and uncompromising opposition to each other. The most ardent Royalists emigrated with the hope of joining foreign forces and of returning to invade France to re-establish the power of the King. These nobles with the King's brothers formed an army at Coblentz on the Rhine. In France the liberals had lost faith in the King and the newly elected left were radicals, mostly Girondists, whose ideas were penetrated with republicanism. The Commune of Paris was already a strong force for insurrection. Necker was dismissed in October; La Fayette was no longer popular because he had defended the King, and Narbonne as Minister of War was preparing the French army to be able to resist the invaders.

The threat of foreign intervention incited the multitude to take the reins of government into its violent hands. Its leaders were Danton, Marat, and Robespierre. On April 20, 1792, France declared war on the coalition of the *émigrés* and the German princes and Austria. Unfortunately, its three armies were ill-organized; many of its aristocrat officers had emigrated. The early battles were defeats for the French.

Oath of the Federation

The third anniversary of the Fall of the Bastille, July 14, was celebrated by the Oath of the Federation at the Champs de Mars. Madame de Staël describes the Queen, "In splendid dress, but with eyes sore from weeping." The King went to the foot of the altar to swear his oath for the second time to "that Constitution of which the relics were about to crush the throne." She adds, "A crowd of children followed the King, with exclamations, children as yet unconscious of the crime with which their fathers were to sully themselves."[5] He returned to his seat beside the Queen and his children. After that the people saw him no more.

The government now passed into the hands of the Girondists, with Mme Roland as its guiding spirit—or fury. It was Mme Roland who symbolized the revolutionary equality to the lower classes. It was she, not Mme de Staël, who was influenced by Rousseau. In 1771 she visited a relation of hers in Paris, a lady-in-waiting to the Dauphiness, Marie Antoinette. Madame Roland observed the luxury, the frivolity, and the easy living of the aristocracy. She went home to Lyons with bitterness and hate in her heart at the contrast between court life and what she knew at home. It was fanatic Mme Roland who spurred on the regicides in 1793 and who cried, "Even a father should not be deterred by any feeling of mercy when the public good is in question."[6] Arriving in Paris in 1791, she became the driving force of the Gironde party, but she, too, eventually fell under the blade of the guillotine during the bloody excesses of factionalism.

The Riot of June 20, 1792

Twenty thousand men marched on the Tuileries where the royal family was in residence on June 20, 1792. They represented the feelings of the people, who felt themselves betrayed by the defeat and disorganization of their unseasoned soldiers. They wanted to frighten the King into signing the Assembly's decrees against recalcitrant priests[7] and fugitive aristocrats. Louis faced the mob with courage and promised nothing. The mob was satisfied with the gesture of placing the red Phrygian bonnet, the cap of liberty, on the King's head.

It was at this ill-timed moment that the Duke of Brunswick, the Prussian commander-in-chief, proclaimed in July, 1792, that he would destroy Paris if Louis were harmed. This announcement caused a serious uprising in Paris. The forty-eight sections of the Paris Commune came under the power of the radical lower class. On August 10 the rabble again marched on the Tuileries, and bloody fighting resulted. The King, seeking refuge in the Assembly, was suspended from his functions and was, with his family, placed in the prison of the Temple.

A new *régime* had to be set up, that of the Convention, but hysteria swept the country. La Fayette, who had tried to defend the King and quell the disorders, had to flee for his life.

Madame de Staël in Danger

Madame de Staël's friends, the liberal aristocrats, were proscribed. In the events of these first days of the Terror Mme de Staël revealed her courage and her selfless generosity. She knew that Narbonne and other friends of hers were defending the King that night of August 10 at the Tuileries. She ventured fearlessly into the rue du Bac only to be turned back at the Seine by guards who told her of the killing going on "over there" (the Tuileries). She succeeded in hiding Narbonne and another friend in her house.

In *Considerations* she relates her own experience of the Terror.[8] One morning her home, the embassy, was subjected to search by members of the Commune, composed of ignorant, uneducated commoners.

I began by alarming these men as much as I could on the violation of the rights of nations of which they were guilty, by searching the house of an Ambassador; and as their knowledge of geography was not extensive I persuaded them that Sweden was a power which could threaten them with an immediate invasion, being situated on the frontiers of France. I had the courage, with anguish in my heart, to jest with them on the injustice of their suspicions. Nothing is more agreeable to men of this class than a tone of pleasantry, for even in the excess of their fury against the upper ranks, they feel a pleasure in being treated by them as equals.

The searchers left, and through a friend, a German Dr. Bollman, she enabled Narbonne to reach England. She herself remained to get news of her friends and to be of help to them despite the serious danger to herself. Jaucourt and Lally Tollendal, intelligent liberals, were in prison. Her effort to free them shows her clever mind as well as her fearlessness. She examined a list of all the official members of the Paris Commune and saw on it the name of Manuel, who, she remembered, had dabbled in literature with a publication of Mirabeau's letters. She wrote to him for an audience, which was granted at seven in the morning—"A rather democratic hour," she remarked. She talked of the fragility of popularity and mentioned that he himself might suffer proscription some day and need a friend. Jaucourt and Lally were excellent men, she said, of service to France. Manuel agreed to help her, and the two prisoners were freed.

However, this was not the end of her adventures. When she left Paris for Coppet she planned to take with her the Abbé de Montesquiou. On the day of departure the alarm bells in Paris were ringing wildly, but she decided she must keep to her plan. She fancied that she would be unmolested and she left openly with her coach-and-six.

"Scarcely had my carriage advanced three steps when, at

the noise of the whips of the postilions, a swarm of old women, who seemed to issue from the infernal regions, rushed my horses, crying that I ought to be stopped, that I was running away with the gold of the nation, that I was going to join the enemy, and a thousand other invectives still more absurd."[9]

The mob surrounding her coach forced her to drive to the section of her Paris quarter. As she stepped from her carriage she whispered to a servant to go inform the Abbé Montesquiou what had happened. When her passports were examined by the chairman of the Commune he noted that one person was absent. She was ordered to the Hôtel de Ville, where Robespierre and his associates were trying cases. She had to cross half of Paris in her carriage, and this took her three hours. The crowds were shouting along the way, "Death, death!" Her fine clothes and coach aroused their fury. The gendarme with her in her coach noted that she was pregnant and told her that he would defend her.

Alighting at the Place de Grève opposite the Hôtel de Ville, she found her courage increased by the "expression of atrocity" on the crowd's faces. She ascended the steps where three days earlier so many had been massacred. On each side of her was a line of guards with pikes. One of them thrust his pike at her, but the gendarme with her raised it with his sabre. She wrote that, had she fallen at that moment, her life would have been forfeited, "For it is in the nature of common people to respect what still stands erect."[10]

The hall was crowded with women and children shouting, "Vive la nation!" She showed her passports as Ambassadress of Sweden. Suddenly Manuel appeared, surprised to find her in such a situation. He made himself responsible for her to the Tribunal, took her to his office, and locked her and her servant inside. From the window they could see "the assassins returning from the prisons with their arms bare and bloody, uttering horrible cries."[11]

In the square, mounted on the box of her coach there was a tall man who was keeping pillagers away. She recognized him as Santerre, the brewer who had helped in her father's distribution of corn to the Paris populace.

That night Manuel took her home. The next day a guard from the Commune, Tallien, came to escort her to the barrier. She arrived safe but exhausted in Coppet on September 7. Two and a half months later (November 20) she gave birth to Albert, her second son by Narbonne.

Plan to Join Narbonne

For Germaine the separation from Narbonne was unbearable anguish. It is portrayed in her passionate letters. To this liaison, and especially to her open exhibition of it to the world, her father and mother were unalterably opposed. Her mother prophesied what was later to take place, that she would be abandoned by her lover.[12] Her passionate resolve to join him in England or to take her own life shocked them. Harsh family quarrels and violent arguments ensued during the months before her departure for England. Necker, tired of the painful scenes, was finally able to succeed in a compromise agreement. Germaine was to remain with the family in Rolle for three months; then if she still felt so passionately attached to Narbonne, he would not oppose her separation from de Staël and her plans to journey to England. Madame de Staël's *Lettres à Narbonne* give evidence of these family scenes, of her fear for Narbonne's life and of her determination to join him in England. Narbonne had written from exile to the Convention that he would return to testify on behalf of his king. He went so far as to publish in London a short defense of Louis XVI, but it succeeded only in arousing greater hatred.

In late December Germaine announced to her family that she was going to Geneva for a short visit. From Geneva she made her way to Paris and her friend, Mathieu, accompanied her to the port of Boulogne.

Abandonment—Juniper Hall

Early in January, 1793, the very month of King Louis's execution, Mme de Staël arrived safely in England to join Narbonne and the little group of *émigrés*, her friends. She rented Juniper Hall, a country house in Surrey, not far from London, where she could have her friends around her. There were in the group Louis de Narbonne, Talleyrand, Mathieu, de Jaucourt, Mme de la Châtre, General d'Arbley, and Dr. Bollman. It was the latter who wrote of Mme de Staël at Juniper Hall, "This Staël woman is a genius, an extraordinary, eccentric woman in everything she does. She sleeps only a very few hours, and is uninterruptedly and fearfully busy all the rest of the time. . . . Whilst her hair is being dressed, whilst she breakfasts, in fact during a third of the day she writes. She has not sufficient quiet to look over what she has written, to improve it or finish it, but even the rough outpourings of her active mind are of the greatest interest, and contain fragments of the finest perception and the most lively force."[13] This "writing" was her work, *The Influence of the Passions on the Happiness of Individuals and Nations.*

The French *émigrés* had a horse and a small chaise and took turns riding through the countryside in it. They made friends with the neighbors, the Burney sisters and the Locks who were friends of Joshua Reynolds, Thomas Lawrence, and the late Dr. Johnson. Fanny Burney and General d'Arbley fell in love and were married a year later. Evenings they spent in gay conversation; after dinner Mme de Staël would read to the group parts of her work on *The Passions*, which she had begun. Thus the little group kept up its spirits and hid its anxieties over events in France.

Events in France

Events in France were more and more heartbreaking. The King had been placed on trial. In October, 1792, Necker had offered to defend the King and had published his *Mémoire Justificatif de Louis XVI.* Because of this loyalty, the Convention sequestered his properties, and he was put on the list of enemies of the Republic. In England, Narbonne tried in vain to get Pitt to intervene. The Convention accused the King of treasonable communication with the enemy and sentenced him to death. On January 21, 1793, Louis XVI was guillotined, to the horror of all Europe, and especially of England. On February 1, England declared war on France.

In spite of the horrors in France and in spite of Narbonne's coolness, Mme de Staël enjoyed three of the best months of her life in the companionship of her friends at Juniper Hall. In February the political atmosphere in England became hostile to the revolutionists and, despite her efforts in London to explain her constitutional ideas, she and her friends were under increasing suspicion.[14] In March her father sent her cousin, Mme Necker de Saussure, to bring Germaine home.

Suzanne Necker was ill and needed Germaine. Her father shut off Mme de Staël's sources of money, and she returned to her home duties. The Baron de Staël, her husband, was back in Coppet, his debts having been paid by Necker. De Staël recognized Gustave, now three years old, and Albert, seven months of age, as his sons. For a time there was an understanding between husband and wife.

Two months after Germaine's return, Suzanne Necker died. Suzanne had told her, "I die of the grief which your guilty and public liaison has caused me . . . it is by the care you will give to your father that you will gain my forgiveness in heaven."[15]

Germaine could not grieve deeply for a mother from whom there had never been deep affection, but rather opposition and disapproval. Between father and daughter, however, there had always been a close and generally happy understanding. When they were together, she stimulated him; when absent from him, her letters were full of anecdotes and descriptions. He understood her need for society, for new things. She respected his opinions and consulted him on domestic details and on the upbringing of her children.[16] It was his sermons that she read to her children on Sunday. It was the example of his life she held up to them.

Besides the sympathy for her father's deep grief in the loss of her mother, Mme de Staël now experienced a growing and bitter consciousness of her lover's abandonment. Her letters to Narbonne in England are passionate love letters, beseeching him to come to Switzerland. Narbonne, however, after the death of his king, no longer shared the idealistic, liberal ideas of Germaine.[17] His was a nature motivated by public opinion; hers, by scorn for convention, which seemed to her to limit creative genius. Narbonne could owe her his life and accept her financial support, but he could not tolerate her dominating kind of love. His case foreshadows Germaine's second shattering love affair, that with Benjamin Constant.

Counts Ribbing and De Pange

In the meantime, in Switzerland, Germaine met and was attracted to Count Adolf Ribbing, a handsome, blond Swede, exiled for his part in the assassination of Gustavus III of Sweden. This short affair was overshadowed by her passion for a man of intellect and enthusiastic ideas which coincided with her own. This man was the handsome young aristocrat, François de Pange. He did not reciprocate her affection, but married his beloved young cousin, Mme de Sérilly, widowed by the guillotine. His ideas, however, expressed in his manuscript, *Essay on the Causes and the Effects of the Progress and Decadence of Literature,* doubtless had an influence on her *Of Literature Considered in its Relations to Social Institutions.*[18]

The Years 1793-1794

The year 1793 was a difficult year for Germaine, as it was for France. The Reign of Terror was in full swing. Madame de Staël characterized it as the time when France was descending, "like Dante from circle to circle always lower in Hell."[19] The years 1793 and 1794 seemed to her to be taking only one direction, that of "making one half of the nation butcher the other half." The execution of Mme Elizabeth in May, and of the Queen in October, and the judicial murders of great men like Condorcet, Lavoisier, Bailly, and Malesherbes, were the work of fear and suspicion.

Reflections on the Trial of the Queen

It was in August, 1793, that Germaine wrote her *Reflections on the Trial of the Queen,* addressed to the Tribunal in Paris. This fervent defense of the Queen is a protest against outrageous brutality and injustice. It is a cry of generous sympathy from her heart for an unfortunate woman who had hated her, yet it only gained her enemies in Paris. In her appeal she admitted hatred for France's traditional enemy, Austria, but defended the Queen's character, her courage in suffering, her maternal love for her children, and her loyalty to her husband.

Her appeal to the people was emotional. "Don't you know

that what is written in letters of blood will be read by the universe?"[20] "You govern by death; the strength which is lacking in the nature of your government you find in terror, and there, where a throne existed, you have raised a scaffold. . . .[21] Woe to the people which could be neither just nor generous; not for such will liberty be preserved."[22] She addressed the last page of her appeal to all women of all countries and of all classes. "I turn once more to you women: for if her tender motherhood were struck, you all would be victims. . . . Your sway will be lost forever once ferocity reigns. . . . Defend the Queen with all the weapons nature has given you." Herold calls it a "manifesto for freedom."

During these tragic months Germaine at Coppet used all the means at her disposal to save her friends from the guillotine. She set up a secret rescue agency. Mathieu, Jaucourt, Malouet, la Princesse de Noailles, la Duchesse de Broglie—all were saved by her generosity. She felt that her affections had nothing to do with her opinions; that duties of friendship were increased by the hour of danger. The obvious faults in her virile, exuberant character may perhaps be forgiven by virtue of her never failing generosity and benevolence toward others and by her utter lack of personal hatred for those who abused her.

In 1794 after her shattering experience with Narbonne she wrote two rather unimportant works. The first, *Epître au Malheur* (*Epistle to Misfortune*), was a versified story of two lovers at the foot of the guillotine. The discipline of verse did not suit her natural lively spirit.[23] Sainte-Beuve considered the *Epistle* a mediocre literary effort. *Zulma*, the second work, was a story of two passionate and tragic lovers, which she wrote to free herself from her own experience with Narbonne. The heroine of *Zulma* kills her false lover and enters the passionate plea in her defense that "love is above laws, above men's opinions; it is the truth, the flame, the pure element, the foremost idea of the moral world." Judging the exaggeration of such a statement we must take into account the violence of Germaine's passion when she thus expressed herself.

In her early works and in *Zulma,* as well as in her novels, *Delphine,* 1803, and *Corinne,* 1807, Mme de Staël expressed a vehement protest against the frivolity and refined cynicism around her. Her tragic heroines were gifted, superior women of refined sensibility and deep passions like herself. She was perhaps unconsciously justifying herself, as well as attacking an artificial society which was oppressive to women. Her chief occupation, besides rescuing her friends from death during this unhappy year, was to continue work on the *Passions*. The study and the research necessary to its creation were to bring her consolation, if not comfort. Hers was not a nature which could stagnate in grief or inaction.

Reflections on Peace

In July, 1794 when Robespierre and his *régime* were shattered, Mme de Staël wrote her *Reflections on Peace* and addressed the first part to William Pitt of England, whom she called the "tutelary genius of the Powers" (*génie tutélaire des Puissances*). The second part she addressed to the French people. She warned Pitt that the ruin of France would carry with it the ruin of Europe. France needed rest. Opposed, she would fight even harder; left in peace, time would weaken the fearful fanaticism of the political religion called equality.[24] She still held to her hope and ideal: "Pity is not dead nor man dedicated to the destruction of man nor is atheism become the superstition (religion) of the people."[25]

Peace was the cry of the land, which was weary of slaughter, the cry of reason and humanity, but there would be no return to the old *régime* whether a republic succeeded or there was a return to a limited monarchy.

Her second pamphlet, *Reflections on Internal Peace*, published in 1795, is eloquent. Part I is directed to the consideration of a limited monarchy. To what king, friend of liberty, could one turn, she asks. Could one rely on him to respect restrictions set by the people? His partisans would retain the same fanaticism and factions. She explores the subject in some detail then turns to consider the republican form of government which she favors.[26] Only in a state of peace can France work out the republican form. Fear and distrust and suspicion of a repetition of the past excesses in the name of liberty are the chief enemies. The need is for leaders of high character. A republican government favors the development of talent. She does not for a moment approve of the existing system or the men in charge of it since the days of 1792. She pleads for the conciliation of all parties and pardon to permit the return of the *émigrés*. She would raise the standard of living of the poor and give them greater means for acquiring property. Property should be the basis for participation in government, because it ensures stability.

She believed that political liberty was to be distinguished from civil liberty, which belonged to all. In civil liberty there was no distinction; all would benefit alike from equal taxation and from legal forms of arrest and trial. As for the legislative process, she advocated a bicameral system and an executive without the absolute veto. She considered the English system but recognized that there was no absolute system of government which should not be modified by local circumstances.[27]

Mme de Staël's passionate appeal was for peace and security without which France could not return to prosperity and establish a just constitution. Sainte-Beuve commented on the *Reflections de la Paix*: "There is an inspiration of antiquity in this figure of a young woman who springs forth to address a people, her foot placed on the still smoking ruins."[28] Mme de Staël saw clearly, even in 1795, that if France were to return to a limited monarchy it would necessarily pass through a military government. Was not this a prophecy of Napoleon?

The important facts that explain Mme de Staël's political beliefs and activities were her undying faith in a constitutional republic as a guarantee of liberty and her constant dream of perfectibility, founded on her study of man's history. Even the blood bath of the Terror, which drew her tears and shook her confidence in life, did not subvert her strong faith in the progress of man and of his institutions.

CHAPTER 5

Benjamin and Germaine

EXILED by the government of the Republic in 1795 for meddling in its affairs, Germaine retired to Coppet. There she worked on *The Influence of the Passions on the Happiness of Individuals and Nations.* Benjamin Constant, her new companion in intellect and love, was with her. He was a significant stimulus to her ideas and personality and their conversation was a constant fireworks of wit and ideas. To Benjamin she was a vital, invigorating force.

Their meeting on the highway one fateful September afternoon of 1794 was a casual meeting, but it did not remain so. The fact is that Constant went to see her at Coppet, missed her there, but overtook her carriage on its way to Rolle. His fascinating talk earned him an invitation to ride with her. Despite his unprepossessing appearance, as a tall, gangling, pale-faced redhead, he fascinated Germaine. Here began what has been called "The most eloquent love affair in history."[1]

Benjamin Constant

Benjamin, a former child prodigy, was almost twenty-seven years old, with great gifts of intelligence and good connections. His life, however, had been a succession of adventures, pranks, and travels resulting in a disillusioned, sick cosmopolite. He had the faults of his time—gambling, dueling, and cynicism.[2]

He spoke several languages, had a good classical background, and was exceedingly intelligent. For several years his feminine friend and counselor had been Mme de Charrière, a disillusioned, bitter, and ironical woman twenty years older than himself. Her philosophy was to take what life offered, but not ask of it joys which few men can give or maintain.

Constant, by this time a mocking, skeptical soul, found a new life in his friendship for Germaine. To Mme de Charrière he wrote, "I believe she is very active, very imprudent, very talkative, but kind, confiding and giving herself up in good faith . . . a combination of astonishing and attractive qualities, so much brilliance and systematic benevolence, so much generosity, such gentle and courteous manners in society with so much charm, simplicity, and easy in familiar intercourse. She is the second woman I have found who could replace the whole universe for me. . . . She is a creature apart, a superior being, such as one meets perhaps once in a century."[3]

Germaine's Influence on Constant

Under Germaine's influence Constant became an enthusiastic and brilliant talker. He left behind his blasé, mocking personality and came to life. He called on her daily, but she did not respond to his impetuous advances. His physique and his manners, which seemed awkward and unattractive to her after the smooth, handsome elegance of Narbonne, Mathieu, and Talleyrand, did not attract her. To break down her resistance he tricked her with an emotional midnight scene of attempted suicide in his room at the château. He called for her piteously. When she finally burst in on the assembled household, he kissed her arms and told her with passion, "You are calling me back to life!" She returned to her room. Although she afterward washed her arms with eau de Cologne, her interest in Benjamin was captured.

Constant wrote in *Cécile*, his autobiographical story, "The perfect conformity of our minds was such that always, when we were together, we had to quarrel or agree, and when we had exhausted our physical strength in argument, a sense of closeness suddenly followed the most appalling storms."[4]

It was an association that was to last through many storms and through many later attempts to escape from it on Constant's part. The story was told by Constant himself in the novel *Adolphe* with lucid self-analysis. He realized that beneath all Germaine's egoism and possessiveness, beneath her efforts to manage and manipulate him, her devotion to him was sincere.[5] Their child was Albertine de Staël, born June 9, 1796.

It was Germaine who inspired Constant's two pamphlets, one concerning law versus arbitrary government, the other dealing with the effects of the Terror, in which he said, "Nothing can justify a crime."[6]

Napoleon Arrives on the Scene

This first year of the association of Benjamin and Germaine saw the establishment of the new Constitution of Year III(1795),[7] with its executive power given to a directory of five. The legislature consisted of two houses, the Council of the Ancients, and The Five Hundred. In October the Royalists managed an uprising and marched on the Tuileries where the Convention was sitting. Barras, head of the Committee of Public Safety, called on a young captain of the army, Napoleon Bonaparte, to head the troops and suppress the uprising. Only six months later Bonaparte was commander-in-chief of the troops in Italy. His campaigns in Italy were a complete success. He made his own terms with the defeated Italians without consulting the Directory. Here was, perhaps, the first evidence of his powerful will to rise to power.

Mme de Staël, held suspect as a friend of Royalists, was still exiled by the Directory from Paris, but her passionate love for Benjamin Constant sustained her. For a year she had to be content with life in Coppet, bored by her father's conversation and comforted by Benjamin Constant. This was the time when she completed *The Influence of the Passions on the Happiness of Individuals and Nations*. She could read and discuss its ideas with Necker and Constant. Her great complaint was the lack of diverting company. The French government, however, kept a close watch on her activities, and had issued the order to jail her if she stepped into France.

When *The Influence of the Passions* was published in 1796, she and Constant left for his Abbey of Hérivaux outside Paris, which had recently been outfitted by a loan from Necker. They spent a quiet winter there, this time threatened as Republican sympathizers by the political change to Royalist ascendancy in the elections of the spring of 1797. Mme de Staël's husband was again (since 1796) in his official position as Ambassador of

Sweden. In June Mme de Staël returned to the embassy in Paris to give birth to her daughter, Albertine.

It was not long, however, before she was again active in her effort to save the Republic from the pressure by the director executives to overthrow the Constitution. Through her efforts a new cabinet was formed, and Talleyrand was appointed Minister of Foreign Affairs.[8] To save the political situation an appeal was made to Napoleon in Italy for backing from the army against those suspected of conspiring against the Republic. Napoleon, in July, made a proclamation to the army in Italy, insisting that it must pacify France. He sent General Augerau to Paris with twelve hundred men.

Germaine at this time was enthusiastic over the victorious general, the "little Corsican." She had written to him in Italy letters of admiration for his victories.

Reversal of Government

On September 4, 1797, a tragic reversal of government took place. Augerau's army surrounded the deputies in the Tuileries, and an authoritarian *régime* was set up, for which Germaine was falsely attacked from all sides. Deputies were deposed; anticlerical laws of the Terror were revived; the press was put under police censorship, and opposition newspapers were closed. The greatest injustice was the deportation of one hundred and sixty-five citizens to the hellhole of French Guiana. Mme de Staël saved as many of the proscribed as she could. For herself she was fearless, continuing her visits in Paris and her conversations as usual. This *coup d'état* prepared the way for that of November 9 with Napoleon coming to prominence.

On December 6, 1797, Mme de Staël met Napoleon for the first time. He was there posing as a man of letters and peace. She found herself ill at ease in his presence, and he showed his dislike of her. She had hoped to charm him as she had other men, but he remained cold and uninterested. Not daunted, she asked him to her house. He did not come. She was not used to rebuffs and in her mind lay the suggestion of a partnership of power. Napoleon, however, disliked women of intellect and thought her mad. He was frightened by her admiring exuberance.

The story is told that at a reception he approached a woman famous for her beauty and intelligence. "Madame," he said, "I do not like women to concern themselves with politics." The woman replied, "You are quite right, General, but in a country where women's heads are removed, it is only natural they may want to know why this is being done."[9]

Napoleon and Madame de Staël

Napoleon's reaction to Mme de Staël was at first coldly polite; with the years it became coarse, and finally ferocious. The more she saw of him, the less confidence she felt. "I had a confused feeling that no emotion of the heart could act upon him. He regards a human being as an action or a thing, not as a fellow creature . . . for him nothing exists but himself; all other creatures are ciphers."[10]

She felt his cold, calculating nature, and was disturbed. Compassion could not throw him off his course, nor could the charm of any person, nor the claims of any religion, nor the belief in any idea. Napoleon, for his part, warned her not to meddle. "Tell her she must never stand in my way. If she does I'll smash her. I'll break her. The only practical thing for her to do is to keep her mouth shut."[11] This her nature and ideas did not permit her to do. She spoke out in her writings as well as in her *salon*. Between 1800 and 1810 she wrote two novels, *Delphine* and *Corinne*, an analysis of *Of Literature in Its Relations to Social Institutions*, and a tome on Germany. Unfortunately for her, Napoleon found in each one, implied, though sometimes unintentional, criticism of his *régime*.

The duel thus engaged lasted for fourteen years of exile. The struggle was between two strong natures, between conflicting ideas and ideals.[12]

Historical Events Summarized: 1798-1812

The events of these years of Napoleon's ascendance can be rapidly summed up. The Egyptian campaign in 1798, in which Lord Nelson defeated the French fleet, was carried out unsuccessfully. Napoleon returned to Paris, where he and his soldiers

effected a final *coup d'état,* which put him on the first rung of
the power ladder. He was established as First Consul with two
colleagues. The two legislative bodies of government had only
a deliberative voice, no power to make laws. By careful maneu-
vers and rewards Napoleon established his rule of order. A
plebiscite named him Consul for Life in August, 1802. By the
same year he had made treaties of peace with all the enemies
of France (though he was to break them two years later) and
had restored financial confidence. His invasion of Switzerland
to liberate it and gain the treasury of Berne recouped French
finances from the disastrous Egyptian campaign. In 1802 he
established the Concordat[13] with the Church of Rome; the
Legion of Honor[14] the same spring. The carriages and pomps of
the old court were revived. Under his *régime* the Bank of
France was organized; the University of Paris was established
with thirty-two lycées, as was the famous Code Civil,[15] which
endured for over a hundred years.

By 1802 Napoleon had a whole class of society devoted to his
fortunes, not only the military, but the clergy and the returned
aristocrats. As emperor he set up a court of princes, chamber-
lains, and marshals. Even the Pope was forced to come to Paris
to consecrate the new dynasty December 2, 1804.

After recognizing the good measures of Napoleon's *régime,*
Mignet, the historian, wrote, "The nation was in the hands of the
great man or the despot; it rested with him to preserve it or
enslave it. He preferred the realization of his selfish projects,
and preferred himself to all humanity."[16] On May 18, 1804, by a
vote of the Senate ratified as usual by a plebiscite, he became
Emperor of the French. He restored the pomp and etiquette of
the former royal court.

For nearly fifteen years Napoleon and his generals won victory after victory with enormous armies in campaigns designed
to bring Europe under French control. Only England in its
island state remained untouched. At one time Napoleon had
even considered invading England, and for this purpose ships
had been prepared at Boulogne.

Defeat of Napoleon

At last after years of victories abroad and triumphs at home, Napoleon's ambition overreached itself. The winter of 1812 saw the ghastly retreat of the French from Moscow. October 1813 saw the final defeat at Leipzig of this French military genius. Napoleon abdicated April 1, 1814, and was sent to his island prison of Elba. France at last breathed a profound sigh of relief.

CHAPTER 6

Essay on Fiction *and*
Influence of the Passions

THE *Essay on Fiction* and the work on *The Influence of the Passions on the Happiness of Individuals and Nations* may be considered together since they belong to the same general period. Larg calls them "her two masterpieces."[1] It was Mme de Staël's thesis that literature could lift man above the misery of his life. The creations of the imagination can divert from sorrow, can strengthen man to meet the inevitable trials of human existence. This she proved during the years of 1794-95 in her own experience. By the time she was twenty-eight years old she had passed through a great and passionate storm in her own life, and in the revolutionary Terror.

She felt that the political problem was a moral problem based on the influence of the passions on man. She must examine these in their relation to the happiness of individuals and of governments. She had begun the first portion at Juniper Hall, but the horrible events of the Terror had interrupted her work for months. This first part is personal; the second part is political and historical. Exiled from Paris, she now organized a daily discipline of study and writing. Virgil, Homer, Spenser, Milton, Burke, Swift, and Montesquieu kept her thoughts occupied.[2] At first irksome, this study gradually freed her spirit.

Purpose of Fiction

"There is no faculty more precious to man than his imagination," she wrote in the *Essay on Fiction*.[3] "Human life seems so full of misfortune and grief that man needs its distractions, happy memories and pleasant creations. Writers bring these to man, and thus they work for the human race. They not only amuse but also have an influence on moral ideas. To entertain is the chief purpose of fiction. The moral must be hidden or embellished with what moves the heart."[4] Her literary analysis and judgment are mature.

She divided fiction into three classes: one, the miraculous or allegorical; two, the historical; three, where all is invented and imitated, but probable. Her thesis was that novels should take life as it is, with "finesse, eloquence, profundity and morality." She disliked the miraculous, but approved in general of allegories which mixed humor and philosophic ideas, such as Swift's *Tale of the Tub*, *Gulliver's Travels*, and some of Voltaire's philosophic tales, but she warned of their danger of fatiguing or losing the reader.[5]

She Points the Way to New Subjects

Fielding's and Richardson's novels, she wrote, possessed invented situations but followed real life, and thus appealed to the reader. The fact that the state of the novel was inferior came from the inferior authors who heaped up insipid works.[6] A well-conceived novel was one of the finest productions of the human spirit for its moral influence. Moreover, she felt that the subject for novels should be broadened from the usually accepted one of the portrayal of love. The novel should treat of other passions such as ambition, pride, avarice, and vanity; thus she pointed the way for later novelists. These subjects came to flower in the writings of Stendhal and Honoré de Balzac.

She named several novels as masterpieces, among them *La Princesse de Clèves*. She also prophesied the psychological novel, the study of the inner movements of the soul which would appear so real that the reader would sense them as true.[7] "The novelist," she wrote, "should add a dramatic touch which, instead of falsifying the effect, would heighten it, as in the painter's art." The power of fiction lay in the gift of evoking the emotions.

Above all, a book was a good companion. It was a comfort, especially to people who felt themselves in grief and sadness (as she did) in "the desert of life." A good book lifted a man out of himself and thus gave him true happiness and pleasure, the only one to which human nature was susceptible.[8]

Influence of the Passions

The work on *The Influence of the Passions*, published in 1796, is concerned with the happiness of individuals and nations as affected by the passions. She has reflected on the unhappy, even tragic, influence of the passions on society. She has the awful picture of ruined France before her as well as her own tragic experience. Part I is developed in three sections, each with several chapters, of which the more important subtitles are as follows: Love of Glory, Ambition, Vanity, Love, Envy and Revenge, Party Spirit (partisan spirit), Crime.

The second section of Part I treats of friendships, filial, paternal, and conjugal affection, and religion. The third section is concerned with the resources to be found within oneself, such as philosophy, study, and benevolence, which diminish the influence of the passions.

Mme de Staël planned a second part to her book which would examine ancient and modern governments in relation to the influence of the passions on the body politic. She would endeavor to find the cause of the birth, duration, and destruction of governments. She would end her work with reflections on the nature of representative constitutions. This second part (Part II) she never accomplished, but her introduction gives a rather full discussion of ideas as she planned to develop them. "If men," she wrote, "succeeded individually in mastering their passions, the systems of government would be simplified and complete independence attained. It is the passions of men which make necessary the sacrifice of man's liberty to keep order."[9]

Happiness

In *The Influence of the Passions* she first defines happiness.

"Happiness, such as it is hoped for, is the sum of contradictions; for individuals it is hope without fear; activity without anxiety, glory without calumny, love without infidelity, the imagination which would beautify what we possess, and wither the memory of what we have lost; in short the intoxication of moral nature, the good of all states, of all talents, of all pleasures, separated from the accompanying evil."[10]

She continues with the happiness of nations. For this it would be necessary also, "To conciliate the liberty of the republics with the calm of monarchies; the emulation of talents with the silence of political parties [factions], the military spirit outside with the respect for law within."[11] She did not believe in Utopias. True happiness is unattainable in human life, but what measure of it can be made possible comes through studying how to avoid the worst difficulties. To this aim she dedicated her book. For the individual, happiness meant mastering the passions. For the nations it depended on the degree to which republican liberty, monarchical stability, and the regulation of partisan and military spirit could be fused into a government based on the respect for law. Over and over again appears the theme of moderation and conciliation of opposing forces or parties.

Part I of her work deals, thus, with man and his destiny; Part II, with that of nations. She realized the need for vast research to carry out this second part. The study of different types of government, she felt, could bring out ideas for forming a better one, a constitution of order and liberty. She would put aside all party spirit, all royalist, republican, and Jacobean ideas.

She wrote from her own experience of the malicious misrepresentation of her actions and ideas publicized in pamphlets and magazines. She gave an eloquent picture of unfaithful friends who betray and calumniate. In late 1795 The Directory had exiled her from Paris as a friend of royalist *émigrés* because of her appeal for conciliation in *Reflections on Peace* and because of her influence with members of The Directory whom she invited to her *salon*.

Man, Master or Slave

Mme de Staël calls the passions "This destructive motive force." Man is either their master or their slave. Her object is to offer a system of life which would spare men suffering by discovering how to understand and control the thoughts, the feelings, and the institutions which bring grief.

Her work was born of her own experience and of the painful circumstances of life around her. In it she sought her own consolation as well as that of her fellow men. She wished to spare others the pain she knew. The way of consolation she could point out to others. For herself she could only reap a harvest of melancholy in temporary solitude. This could not satisfy her own need for action, for movement or even glory.

Analysis of Ideas

A brief analysis of the work *The Influence of the Passions* brings out her keen observation and good judgment in the study of man and his works.[12] Love of glory she finds is the greatest spring of action for genius or virtue to serve mankind. It is an intoxicating joy, but evokes criticism in those of mediocre intelligence. Ambition is a very different thing. Its whole aim is to obtain and keep power for itself. It becomes double-faced and double-minded. Ambition is selfish, self-centered, and corrodes a man's character. Only in revolutionary times does such selfish ambition succeed in grabbing power. Revolution relies on physical force, on the fanaticism of certain ideas. The one in power is forced to keep ahead of its tide or fall beneath its inflexible cruelty. Excess is piled on excess.

To the modern reader her discussion becomes, now and then, tiring, because we have accepted her ideas and many of them have become commonplace. The changed condition of women since her day owes much to her work. Her discussion is very personal. A woman, she wrote, who strives with men's ambitions, is resented. Man has willed the limitations of a woman's career, however beautiful her face or broad and forceful her mind.

Her own experience and personality intrude when she complains that a woman, even a genius, cannot live alone; glory cannot satisfy her.[13] She needs to satisfy her need for love as a beloved wife and happy mother does. A famous woman is the object of hate and envy among women who have never had so much as two ideas in their head. Superior women are doomed to unhappiness.[14]

Love she felt was sacrifice.[15] The great joy of living for another gave direction and activity to life. The very thought of losing love brought melancholy and the thought of death. Nothing else in life held equal worth to that of being truly loved.[16] We feel the violence of her emotions.

Women Disinherited by Society

There is a melancholy bitterness in her observations of the society of her times. Nature and society, she wrote, have disinherited half the human race (she means the feminine half). Strength, courage, genius, independence—all belong to men. Youth gives a woman power for a moment, but it is lost for the other half of her life as she grows old. A man receives all that a woman can give, then disengages himself and leaves her to suffer in her emotion, in her pride and agony of spirit. Love is the story of a woman's life; it is an episode in a man's.[17] (This was certainly her own experience.) For women the lasting quality of love is their only happiness. She appeals to women to remain in the path of virtue or they will suffer by man-made worldly opinion. This theme she takes up again in her novel *Delphine* of later date. For women there is the consolation of home duties, of children, of the joy of a mother's love.

Partisan Spirit and the Terror

One of the most interesting chapters in the *Passions* is that on partisan spirit (*esprit de parti*). She saw the danger of intolerance from partisan spirit even in a principled cause. The power of cool reason is lost. Men in a party are united by a common hate, not by esteem.[18] They see only one side of a question, and the truth is hidden from them.[19]

She never agreed that the end justified the means.[20] No one had the right to work evil in order to arrive at good. Time and again she drew examples from the Revolution. For the tyranny of the Robespierre days she could find no excuse, no basis whatever. It was a time outside of nature, even beyond the depths of crime, a monstrosity.

Friendship and Religion

Her chapter on "Friendship" presents a brighter picture. She had risked her life and used her fortune many times to save her friends of whatever opinion and faith they might be. Generosity in the service of her friends redeemed her need to dominate them. I have already told how she saved many from the guillotine, at the risk of her own life. "Religion" brings her comment on the strong faith of those who went to the guillotine unafraid. Faith to her was a gift which could fill one's whole life. Religion, as she knew it, as a creed or doctrine, presented a limited code of generosity and benevolence. The truly virtuous man is he who follows the impulse of his best nature in good deeds.[21]

Thought Is Man's Finest Faculty

Philosophy gives man the power to get outside himself, to observe himself, to think and live.[22] It is a source of happiness for those who like solitude, but solitude only increases the unhappiness of passionate souls by its quiet contrast with the inner tumult. Here Mme de Staël is again thinking subjectively. Only distraction, she said, can weaken the force of a great passion (like hers). This she indulged in as only her restless, unsatisfied soul could do. A melancholy comfort, she continues, could come from the contemplation of all the great misfortunes of history. To her, the thought of the immortality of the soul brought some consolation. The finest faculty of man is this power of thought, for thought is the only faculty which does not speak of dissolution, but leads on, perhaps, to the beginning of eternity.[23]

Thus she concluded that man's happiness would be found in the exercise of his best faculties, in the inner resources of his being. His best faculty was, indeed, that of the mind, of thought.

Benevolence

Her closing chapter dealt with benevolence which, for her, included all the actions of goodness. Benevolence to her was almost a religion.[24] It filled the heart as surely as study busied the mind. She praised the power of compassion and ended her work with an address to the French to be generous in victory.

Larg comments that Mme de Staël is ready to mend her character, to moderate her emotions, but her own advice brings protest from her soul. "If she overcame her passions, she would no longer be herself."[25] There would be no more problems for her, but likewise there would be no more Mme de Staël.

Passions is a book full of noble and stimulating ideas. It analyzes human life with a brilliant and sensitive touch. It suggests different ways to console the troubled soul, from philosophic study to religion. Her thought ranges beyond the individual to include the project of perfecting political institutions to procure happiness for whole nations. Mme de Staël uses the term political science, a subject so widely studied and developed since her time.

CHAPTER 7

Literature Considered in Its Relations to Social Institutions

Germaine and Napoleon

MADAME de Staël was one of the first to see and oppose the direction political events were taking to rob France of her hard-won republican liberty. Her early enthusiasm for Napoleon during his conquests in Italy and the early months after his return to France changed to mistrust, hostility, and fear.[1] With Constant in the Tribunal to speak for the opposition she continued to gather people of influence in her *salon* to discuss the constitution. There was, however, an unbelievable weariness in the people after the exhausting years of discussion and of war. Peace, and a chance to rest, absorbed their thoughts and desires. Napoleon could advance his projects undisturbed. Only Mme de Staël's group offered opposition to them.

When Napoleon sent his brother Lucien to try to conciliate her, he asked, "What does she want? That her father be repaid? All right. To be in Paris? All right." Knowing the price of acceptance, she answered, "It's not what I want but what I think that matters."[2]

Not fully appreciating the power of Napoleon's displeasure as Consul, Mme de Staël urged Constant to speak out for an independent Tribune. The result was unanimous regrets from her guest list at the banquet she had planned to celebrate Constant's victory. She was advised to leave Paris for Saint-Ouen, and Napoleon mounted a harsh press campaign against her. She was attacked bitterly for the errors of her private life.

When Napoleon's brother, Joseph, tried as her friend to persuade her to go to Switzerland, she decided to stay in France and write a book which would win favor and re-establish her.

This book was the amazing *Literature Considered in Its Relations to Social Institutions* (*De la Littérature considérée dans ses Rapports avec les Institutions Sociales*), a volume of over six hundred pages with documented facts, and written in a few months.

It has been considered a plea for the emancipation of women, especially of superior, talented women, as a manifesto of the approaching Romantic movement in France, and as a polemic against Napoleon and military men dominating a nation.[3] It is a proof of her recovery through her studies from the gloom of the years 1794-96. Her thesis is the perfectibility of the human spirit which, in generation after generation, goes forward to a better order. To accomplish this she follows the unequal march of civilization through the ages from the days of Homer to those of the French Revolution, a project of tremendous scope, which does not frighten her bold, inquiring spirit. She penetrates the history of institutions, mores, and literature with an amazing power of analysis and always with her thesis in view. Her cousin, Mme Necker de Saussure, comments on the fact that such a work was conceived in the midst of persecution and exile.[4] It was an event for the thinkers of her day, wrote Sainte-Beuve.[5] "There is scarcely an idea of the nineteenth century which it does not contain in germ."[6]

The Plan of La Littérature

Mme de Staël's plan, explained in the *Discours Préliminaire*, is to examine the principal epochs of literary history. First she intends to assemble some of the general ideas which show the influence of religion, custom, and law upon literature as well as the power that literature can exert on the destiny of man. It will be a research founded on the consideration of facts, not metaphysics, and her hope is to inspire in literature a new strength by the consideration of useful ideas, the love of morality, the ambition of glory, that uplift the soul. She will return again and again in this work to prove her theory of the perfectibility of the human race.

Part I presents a moral and philosophic analysis of the Greek and Latin literatures. It covers seven chapters, beginning with Homer and ending with the reign of the Antonines. Greek poetry, she writes, has not been surpassed in three thousand years. This astonishing success of the Greeks could be an objection, she admits, to her thesis of perfectibility, but she counters this objection by repeating that she is speaking not of the great works of the imagination but of the progress of ideas which goes on forever. Fine arts are not infinitely perfectible because they are the imitation or portrait of physical nature and are thus limited by our senses. There is a fallacy in her argument here.

On the whole she paints an admiring picture of Greek literature, its great tragedies and beautiful poetry. The comedies, those of Aristophanes, she feels are full of vulgarities. Racine, who imitated the Greeks, placed a moral development beside the power of fatalism in his portrayal of passion, whereas the agent in Greek tragedies was an outside supernatural force of some god. Women were given little importance by the Greeks, hence the lack of ability to paint love. She emphasizes the value of the republican form of government which made Aristotle's philosophic work so great but asserts that Greek independence was destroyed by the excessive love of amusements. She felt that the greatness of the English tragedies and of Molière's comedies in contrast with the Greeks showed the progress of the human spirit.

Mme de Staël prefers the Romans to the Greeks because they brought to perfection what the Greek culture had sown in all the corners of the earth. We feel her eighteenth-century *parti pris* when she praises the Romans for being the first to begin literature with philosophy, and for possessing qualities of reason, practical knowledge, dignity, and balance. Utility was the creating principle of Latin literature; the need to amuse was that of the Greeks. The Roman Empire fell because of its corruption, its emphasis on voluptuousness.

The Middle Ages Were Not the Dark Ages

She continues her analysis with the invasions from the North which brought renewed vigor. Women among the Germanic tribes had a sort of civil equality and brought into literature the subjects of generosity, merit, and humanity. The advent of Christianity brought compassion, goodness, and affection.

She does not agree with the general belief that during ten centuries the human spirit retrograded into darkness (the Dark Ages), and she proves her point by emphasizing the importance of the historic invasions for the spread of culture.

"I do not think that this great work of moral nature has ever been abandoned; in the periods of light as in the periods of darkness, the gradual march of the human spirit has not been interrupted."[7] Christianity was indispensable to civilization in bringing together the bold spirit of the North and the gentle customs of the South. It was the force which developed mental faculties through scholasticism and meditative study. It developed metaphysics and morality. It freed the slaves and raised the value of human life. Emphasizing the equal dignity of all human beings, it made marriage sacred.

Division of Northern and Southern Peoples

One of her most famous generalizations, which she was to repeat and develop in her book *Germany*, was her division of the nations or peoples of Europe into two groups with distinctive literatures. These were the group of Northern peoples on the one hand, the German, Scandinavian, and English people with Ossian as the literary origin, and the Southern peoples, the Greeks, the Romans, Spanish and Italians, on the other hand, with Homer as their source. The characteristics of the northern group were love of liberty, sensitive imagination, and melancholy with a tendency to the mystic. These were reflections of their natural surroundings of forests, clouds, and cold. The south, with its bold sun and bright nature, developed a literature that was light-hearted, form-conscious, brilliant, colorful, imaginative, and sensitive. The north was more adapted to a free, independent people. The Reformation originated there, "the epoch of history which has served the perfectibility of the human race the most efficaciously."

There follow three chapters on English literature, one on German and two on French. The genius of Shakespeare transcends the arbitrary rules of taste. She prefers a work with a dash of genius, though with great faults, to a mediocre work which is perfect in form. Still she reproaches northern literature for placing "scènes ridicules" beside passages of great beauty. The rules of art are determined by the success achieved which then abrogates them, but the rule of good taste is above all rules. Mme de Staël has thus loosened the grip of arbitrary rules but retained the value of good taste. She wonders whether the theater of the Republic will admit the Shakespearean heroes with their faults and the placing of vulgar scenes beside the noble ones. The Romanticists answered for her in the affirmative some years later in the works of Victor Hugo. She feels the great power of Shakespeare's dramas, his delineation of character, of the emotions of love, fear, terror, and especially of pity.

English literature is superior in the depiction of nature, linking it with philosophic ideas. English novels emphasize the portrayal of the affections, the analysis of the heart. English philosophy is scientific, based on abstract calculation as well as pragmatic considerations. "Happy the country," she wrote of England, "where the writers are gloomy, the merchants satisfied, the rich melancholy, and the masses content."

Considering German literature, she writes that it is of recent creation because previous writers were occupied with metaphysics and the sciences and often wrote in Latin. The fact that Germany was divided into several small states without a chief capital city in which distinguished writers could gather influenced the literature. There was no interest in political realities but rather in free philosophic speculation and the analysis of feelings of passion and the sufferings of the soul. She praises Goethe's *Werther* as the outward expression of the German "sickness of the soul," a companion to Jean-Jacques Rousseau's *La Nouvelle Héloïse*. Both were great paintings of passion and its suffering.

She interrupts her analysis to express a rather remarkable judgment. If by some insurmountable misfortunes, France were destined one day to lose forever all hope of liberty, it would be in Germany that the center of enlightened thought, the principles of political philosophy, would at some period be established. Of France she says, "We have founded only hatreds and the friends of liberty march in the center of the nation, with head bowed, blushing for the crimes of one group and calumniated by the prejudices of the other." She appeals to the German nation: Let it never permit an action of which morality cannot approve. Little did she realize what history was to bring when the Germans were aroused from their dormant nationalism.

Part II

In Part II of *Literature* Mme de Staël planned to examine French ideas (*lumières*) and thought and to make some guesses as to the future "if we some day possess republican morality and liberty." This leads to her statement of belief in the perfectibility of the human race.

For nations may cease to exist, but the human race presses on to fulfill the aims it has in view. It pursues an ever ascending path through history. No stagnation, even over the course of centuries, no deviation from the right track prevents the progress of the race, which is determined by intellectual facts and not by outside circumstances only. The individual comes and goes; the idea remains; and to the help of human wisdom come the experience of the generations, the discoveries of genius, and the conquests of knowledge.[8]

We note here an emphasis not on person or leader but rather on ideas and the accumulated wisdom which are expressed by men. Apropos of this accumulated wisdom we find her suggesting a science of politics. She had made a study of Condorcet's statistical studies[9] on probability and devotes several pages to a discussion of their use in predicting a correct government for a people with known characteristics. "Why should we not some day succeed in drawing up tables that would contain the solution for every political issue in accordance with statistical information and precise data collected in every country?"[10] It would probably take modern computers to effect this but nothing is impossible to perfectible man. She warns us that "whenever the calculation made does not agree with morality, the calculation is false. Any calculation that ignores suffering and sentiment is barbaric and false."[11] We are impelled to think of the Nazi attempt at genocide and their practice of experimental medicine on human victims in our century.

In the Preface to the second edition of *Literature* she defends her thesis of perfectibility. For fifty years it has been a common idea held by enlightened philosophers, by Kant, Turgot, and Condorcet. The inventions of the compass and of printing have had much to do with the moral and political progress of the world. And she adds prophetically that if one should some day direct navigation in the air, how different would be the relations of society! Again she warns that the progress of the sciences renders necessary the progress of morality, for by augmenting the power of man one must contain his capacity to abuse that power. "Each time that a nation such as America and Russia progresses, the human race is bettered. Each time a lower class is freed from slavery or indignity the human race is again perfected. It would take a book to refute all the objections made to this thesis and only time and posterity, freed from today's 'petite fureur' will write this book." These are powerful words which have deep meaning for the world today.

In her chapters on French literature Mme de Staël traces the influence of the political institutions of feudalism and absolute monarchy upon literature. The nobles gave the king their loyal submission; the king rewarded by flattery and privileges and punished by censure. It was a delicate situation in which charm of manner and subtlety in the selection of favors reigned. The court's elegance of manner and speech influenced the writers. Thus it was the monarchical institutions and customs which produced French wit, grace, and elegance. In the eighteenth century, after the death of Louis XIV, the pressure of the abuses of power was gradually lightened, and men dared to question political institutions and religion. Literature was no longer only an art to amuse and inform; it became a means, a weapon, for serious change and for this purpose prose is developed.

The last chapters of *Literature* emphasize character in leadership, tolerance and urbanity in men's relations to one another, and a new status for women. As a woman of intelligence and a writer she has suffered cruelly but there will come a time, she says, when women will be given education and civil laws to protect them. It is women who are the source of generosity, humanity, and delicacy in a society. Mme de Staël feels a new character is stirring in French tragedy, the painting of great men of history with sentiments which bring them close to all hearts. Theater must present real life and common circumstances which will heighten the contrast of great effects. The future literature of republican France should have simplicity, naturalness, and decency. She counsels against imitation of the old masterpieces of antiquity. "Il vaut mieux défricher le nôtre," ("It is better to cultivate our own.") a comment repeated by the Romanticists. There will be a return to enthusiasm, she says, to virtue and to the delights of the emotions. There is a higher source for virtue than reason; its author is God.

She ends her book with an impassioned chapter on the indestructible progress of man under the united power of genius and virtue. She reverts to her own personal difficulties and admits that she cannot separate her ideas from her feelings. It is our feelings which cause us to reflect, which alone can give thought a rapid and profound penetration.

Reaction to La Littérature

The publication of this remarkable book in 1800 loosed against Mme de Staël the anger of those who accused her of criticizing France and lauding foreign countries, of rousing revolutionary feeling. She had hoped that it would vindicate her in the eyes of public opinion and of Napoleon as well. The book was, indeed, a success, but Napoleon was furious. He quite unjustly accused her of neglecting her husband, old and ill, but the truth of the matter was that Necker had sent him 18,000 francs to help him return to Sweden when he lost his post as ambassador in 1798. De Staël preferred to remain in Paris in a small apartment on the Place de la Concorde. Two years later Necker received word that de Staël was sick and alone. Necker had sent him 20,000 francs over this period, but de Staël's gambling habits kept him poor. He had made an obligation of an annual pension and had bought a house for Mlle Clairon, an aging actress. To protect their own fortune from the son-in-law's debts the Neckers had granted him a lump sum of 10,000 francs and a modest annual pension. When de Staël could not pay her pension Mlle Clairon sued him and the bailiffs took his furniture. This was too much for M. de Staël and he suffered a stroke. When Germaine early in 1801 went to investigate conditions she found de Staël a paralytic in deep misery. She took him to Coppet with her but he died on the way. She buried him at Coppet and spent six weeks putting his affairs in order, "making up through my care for the sentiments I had been unable to give him."[12]

CHAPTER 8

Delphine

Preface

MADAME de Staël's next literary work after *Literature* was the novel *Delphine*, published in December, 1802. It was in the form of letters, with a preface discussing the novel as a genre. "The proper study of man is man," she wrote, quoting Alexander Pope.[1] "Fiction founded on the lasting truths of life teach man these lessons by giving to the reader the feeling of real life." The fault of French literature was its "sterility, coldness, and monotony."[2] The study of the works of other nations brings new ideas and feelings and invigorates the French natural good taste. Imagination and reason are linked but imagination rises above the limits of reason and still holds to reality. Madame de La Fayette's novel, *La Princesse de Clèves,* was the first good French novel. "It was the first which succeeded in uniting the painting of the brilliant manners of chivalry with the touching language of impassioned affections."[3]

The English novels of the eighteenth century are true masterpieces of the novel, and the Germans, too, had novels of deep sensitivity and truth, although unknown in France. It is good for one people to read the works of another. "By reading the productions of a people whose manner of thinking differs so much from that of the French, the mind is excited by new combinations, and the imagination is animated by the bold flights it condemns as much as by those it approves. In studying these works our authors might succeed in adapting to the French taste, which is, perhaps, the purest in the world, some original beauties which would give to the literature of the nineteenth century a character entirely its own." Is she not giving advance notice of, and to, the Romanticists? This theme, the spread of the works of foreign literatures to enrich the French, recurs again and again in her writings.

The events of the plot in the novel, she feels, must serve only to develop the passions of the human heart, and must retain the illusion of reality. Novels such as *Clarissa, Tom Jones, La Nouvelle Héloïse,* and *Werther* reveal a host of feelings of happiness and sorrow which come from the circumstances of life. "These feelings men cannot and do not communicate to one another in real life."[4]

Mme de Staël spoke of the influence of religious opinions which contributed to the glory of the literature of the eighteenth century. She names admiringly the "uncommon, brilliant and original imagination" of Chateaubriand's *Génie du Christianisme.* She believed that literary work of value received inspiration from the great religious ideas, the existence of God, of the immortality of the soul and their relation to morality. However, she related these ideas to the power of enthusiasm, freed from dogma and man-made conventions.

Delphine was written at the time of the Concordat with Rome and of the religious discussion aroused by Chateaubriand's *Génie du Christianisme.* A change in the divorce law was also in debate at this time.[5] All of these are reflected in the novel but the political events are, in general, referred to only obliquely, as for example, the bloody crimes of the Terror urging Léonce to enlist with the *émigrés.* One letter only discusses politics. De Lebensei, the liberal thinker, expresses some of Mme de Staël's ideas as follows: "It is vain to think of imposing a better system of political institutions on any nation by means of external force. Every time a nation tries to attain liberty I may strongly blame the means it takes but I cannot be uninterested in its goal. Liberty is the first happiness, the only glory of the social order."[6]

Men are impressed today by the examples in England of the respect of the laws for man and of men for the laws. The cause of liberty is ill defended in France, but the hope of liberty can rise only from the principles of the revolution. In the present struggle the factions press their opinions to extremes and "he who begins the war with the single aim of reestablishing order hears said around him: there is rest only in slavery, there is security only in despotism, morality only in prejudices, religion only in such and such a sect, until he is carried away far from his goal, whether he resists or yields to the current. Such is the condition in France that in political life the unfortunate are blamed without pity and the powerful yield obedience without esteem."

Delphine is a living portrait of the aristocratic society of the time. Some of the characters have been recognized as real people, such as Talleyrand, who is portrayed in the scheming, perfidious Mme de Vernon and Narbonne as Léonce.

Plot, Theme, and Method of Delphine

The artificial letter method which Mme de Staël uses makes *Delphine* unattractive to the modern reader. In Mme de Staël's day, however, it was a great success. It revealed unusual psychological analysis and presented her ideas on religion, marriage, and woman's position in society.

The subtitle of the novel is this: "A man must be able to brave opinion; a woman to submit to it." This theme is brought out in her protest in Volume II, page 4: "the hazard of braving the opinion of the world is a critical point for a woman; to attempt it one must, in the language of the poet, have triple brass around the heart; must become insensible to the shafts of calumny, and concentrate within one's self all the warmth of one's sentiments . . . to have the fortitude to renounce the world, to possess the resources which disdain its aid. . . ."

The complicated plot is as follows. Delphine d'Albemarle, young widow of the elderly and wealthy M. d'Albemarle makes a generous gift of part of her fortune to her cousin, Mathilde, to enable her to marry Léonce de Mondoville, half French, half Spanish, whose status-conscious mother requires this for her son. Delphine is influenced by her deep friendship for Mathilde's mother, Mme de Vernon, who is later revealed as the villain of the piece, operating under cover of this friendship.

Léonce meets Delphine before the wedding and falls in love with her, the warm and charming young widow, rather than with his prospective bride. Despite Delphine's efforts to direct his attentions to Mathilde, she falls desperately in love herself with this handsome proud young aristocrat.

A subplot at this point involves Delphine in a generous action to save her friend from a jealous husband. She acts as go-between for Thérèse d'Ervins and her lover M. de Serbellane.

They are discovered at Delphine's home and in the ensuing duel, Thérèse's husband is killed. Delphine protects her friend at the risk of her own reputation. Her friend, Mme de Vernon, promises to inform Léonce of her innocence in the affair but does nothing of the sort; instead she relies on the proud character of Léonce, his sensitivity to honor and especially to public opinion, to condemn Delphine and to agree to hasten the marriage with her daughter. The emotion-filled scene in which Delphine, broken-hearted and disillusioned, watches the wedding from behind a marble column in the church, is reminiscent of *Clarissa Harlow.*

Léonce discovers too late that he has been tricked; that Delphine's generous action was innocent. For a long period the two lovers express a platonic devotion to each other. Delphine, faithful to a promise to Mme de Vernon on her deathbed, controls the passionate desires of Léonce, but finally public gossip poisons the situation. Delphine confesses their love to Mathilde who has somehow remained unsuspecting all this time. Mathilde is about to have a child and begs Delphine to leave Léonce forever.

Delphine departs secretly for Switzerland to take refuge in a convent whose directress just happens to be an aunt of Léonce. She is a cold, dominating Spanish nun who tries in every way to make Delphine in her lonely despair take the sacred vows and thus serve the mother of Léonce. The main thread of the story is interrupted by the appearance of M. de Valorbe, a passionate rejected lover of Delphine. He pursues her for her implied promise to marry him if he would renounce his duel with Léonce. He is pitilessly bitter and uses a treacherous method to get Delphine into his power. His appeal to her for help brings her to his room in the nearby German town of Zell. There is a violent scene interrupted by the arrival of German soldiers who take Delphine into custody.

Only irrevocable vows can now save Delphine's reputation. De Valorbe's letter, which blames himself and justifies her in the eyes of the world, comes too late to save Delphine from taking the vows. To climax her despair Delphine now hears that Mathilde and her baby have died and Léonce is free. When Léonce hears that Delphine is now a nun, his liberal Protestant friend tries to convince him that all is not lost, that the Revolution has abolished convents and religious vows. Delphine and he can be united and live happily on the family property of the Mondovilles in the French Vendée. With permission from the abbess Delphine goes to Baden to recover her health and is joined there by Léonce.

The novel has two endings. In the first Delphine realizes that Léonce will never be able to overcome his fear of dishonor and of public opinion. He leaves hurriedly to join the army of the *émigrés*. Scarcely arrived there, he is captured by a French patrol and is sentenced to death. Delphine entreats the judge to free him but, failing in her plea, she takes poison as she accompanies him to the place of execution. At her death the firing squad in pity refuses to shoot Léonce until he forces them by his insults. The second ending was written three years later because of the criticism lodged against the suicide ending. (In 1813 with more mature judgment, she wrote an article against suicide.) In this second ending the two lovers go to the Mondoville estate where it becomes plain to Delphine that their happiness cannot survive the hostile public feeling against her. She becomes ill and dies in the arms of Léonce, who goes to serve in the Vendean army and is killed in his first military action.

Delphine *and Mme de Staël*

Madame Necker de Saussure made the clever appraisal of the two novels of Mme de Staël as follows: "Corinne is the ideal of Madame de Staël; Delphine is her youthful reality."[7] Germaine is now over thirty years of age, has lived an intense life, both of mind and of passion, always with excess of enthusiasm and its ensuing tragic suffering and disillusionment.

Delphine protests: "When we are deprived of the greatest of all blessings, that is, of a marriage of love, must we extinguish every feeling and become a prey to total insensibility, like so many beings who say that they find themselves at ease?"[8] "What gives me the strength to disdain all appearances and raise myself even above public opinion, is the certainty that I have done no wrong: I do not fear men while my conscience reproaches me with nothing."[9]

Delphine presents again the problem of women's position in

society. Men have more freedom than women outside the
domestic circle. For a woman "there is no happiness in life
except in marriage, in the affection of children, which is never
perfect except when their mother is beloved and cherished."[10]
Through the character of Mme de Cerlèbe, she gives an eloquent
picture of the love of one's children, "their lively imaginations,
their inexhaustible fancies."

Religion

A discussion of religion enters the novel. Mme de Staël expresses her ideas through the liberal de Lebensei. He praises
Protestantism, which he feels is nearer than Catholicism to the
pure spirit of the Gospel, and does not fetter the power of the
understanding.[11] Catholicism imposes a constraint through in-
quisitional terror and indissoluble vows exacted from man. All
men are animated with an ardent desire for happiness, which
should not be represented as a guilty temptation, nor should
it go to extremes. In many circumstances the happiness of others
requires self-immolation.

"Does God require inseparable union?" Delphine asks. "Did
he mean no separation from an insensible, stupid, even criminal
person? Divorce is necessary because of the imperfection of
human nature."[12]

Delphine's passion wrings from her the following eloquent
plea: "Shall I find no distraction of thought, no ideas, however
transient, to cool this fever in my blood even for a few minutes?"
"What consolation can the powers of reason impart? Fortitude,
resignation, patience." It was years before Mme de Staël could
bring herself to practice this resignation and patience. Delphine
reflects that everything that is distinguished in the world has
been persecuted by misfortune, love, virtue, genius. The only
peace and happiness that she can find must be in the devotion
of her life to the welfare of others. This theme recurs in later
writings.

There are several examples of unhappy marriages in *Delphine*
—beautiful young girls married to much older men. In one case,
that of Thérèse d'Ervins, the final solution is renunciation of
the world in a convent. In the case of Mme de Lebensei, the
solution is divorce and marriage to an educated man who

cherishes her and braves public opinion. Of the first solution Delphine asks, "Will not the sentiments of religion be gradually cooled in your breast—the exalted sentiments of a religion which subsists on credulity and enthusiasm alone?"[13]

Mme de Staël's concept of religion was that of Christian morality, not dogmatic creed. She believed in the power of conscience, in the immortality of the soul, a belief which comforted her at her father's death. She could not accept the mystic quietism of a Mme de Krüdener (cf. p. 113). Moreover, her religious feelings came and went. Abel Stevens reports her conversation with Lacretelle on his visit to Coppet in 1802. "If human love draws together all souls, divine love draws together the creature and the Creator, the intelligent atom and the intelligence which fills the universe. All worldly as I am, I have at times some of the experience of Santa Theresa, and these are the best moments of my life. But they are rare with a mind as mobile as it is ardent. Oh! that I could enjoy them more frequently! but I was not born for a contemplative life."[14]

Delphine is an early member of the long line of romantic novels extolling the ecstasies and agonies of the heart. It belongs to the family of *Werther, La Nouvelle Héloïse, Paul et Virginie, Atala,* and *Réné.* With *Corinne* it anticipates the heroines of George Sand, but with a noticeable difference. The latter are women of romantic passion; Delphine and Corinne are much more. They are the superior women of talent and ideas as well as of passion.

In Mme de Staël's characterizations she uses less exterior descriptive detail and more inner analysis of ideas and motives. The following passages may serve as examples.

(Mme de Vernon) "She seems to regard success as everything, and to put little value on the principles of human conduct."

(Mathilde) "Her beauty, which is perfect, will not involve her in any danger, for her virtue will always be supported by the unalterable austerity of her principles . . . she respects all the prejudices and submits to all the rules of society; she will never be exposed to the censure of the world."

(Mme de Marset) "Incapable of procuring herself enjoyment by her friendships, she sought it in her hatreds."

(M. de Serbellane) "His countenance is engaging and dignified; his features have the expression common to the natives of the south of Europe, while from his manner he might be taken for an Englishman. His mind is grave and energetic. He has so complete a command of himself, he does not utter a single involuntary expression."

The picture of Delphine by Léonce is perhaps more descriptive:

She is an inspired being, Delphine. Her voice is animated, her ravishing eyes look toward the heaven as though to take it as witness to her noble thoughts. Her charming arms were naturally placed in the most agreeable and elegant manner. The wind often blew her blond hair into her face; she brushed it away with a grace and casualness which increased her charm.

Delphine animates conversation by putting interest into what she says and into what she hears; no pretension, no constraint; she seeks to please, but only by displaying her natural qualities. All the women I have known have sought to impress others. Delphine is both proud and simple enough to believe herself more loveable when she freely shows what she feels.

Reaction to Delphine

In 1802, when *Delphine* was first published, it was a great success, not only in France but also in England and Germany. When Bonaparte read the digest made of its six hundred pages he fumed that it was immoral and antisocial. He saw the revolutionary sympathies it concealed in certain of its characters, although the political background of 1790-92 was generally absent. He noted her remark in the preface that writers will now express what they consider good and true to a silent but enlightened France, to a future rather than a present time. It could not fail to enrage him.

Mme de Staël wrote a new preface for the second edition in which she defended her moral aim. She was showing how a superior woman is capable of making more mistakes than a mediocre soul unless reason governs her passion. She needed the compassion of society, not its condemnation.

One critic has called *Delphine* "a bad great novel"; in other words, its importance outshines its faults. The hero and heroine are idealized, but most of the other characters stand out as living members of their society. The plot is complicated but handled skillfully despite the difficulty resident in the letter form. There is little attention to nature and its beauties. The central theme is the passionate love of Delphine and her misfortunes in which she is trapped. Léonce serves inversely to express Mme de Staël's protest against the rigor of artificial conventions and public opinion. The ideas concerning women's place, liberty, and tolerance are true today. The novel was the first example of social criticism and anticipates the works of the nineteenth century.

An interesting circumstance is related about the name given to her novel. Mme de Staël was at this time (1802) *persona non grata* with the First Consul, Napoleon. She went to a ball where he was to appear, and was ostracized by the ladies; Mme de Staël has given an evocation of this scene in *Delphine*. Left alone in a corner she was joined by a young woman of courage and heart. As they chatted Mme de Staël asked her name. "Delphine" came the reply. "Oh! I shall try to immortalize it," replied Mme de Staël. She did. The young woman was Delphine, the Comtesse de Custine.[15]

It was the custom of Germaine to spend summers with Necker and her children at Coppet and during the year to make many visits to France to oversee her publications, to conduct business, and above all to visit friends. Now, however, she was definitely exiled from Paris by Napoleon's orders. In her frustration she determined to visit Germany.

CHAPTER 9

Weimar, Italy, and Corinne

BEFORE the Revolution Henri Meister and Grimm[1] were
regular guests in the *salon* of Mme Necker. Grimm returned from Germany in 1774, singing the praises of young
Goethe. Thus Mme de Staël early came in contact with German
writers and thought, at least indirectly. The French did not
study German and knew the German thinkers as scientists,
moralists, and political economists, but not as literary men.

Mme de Staël read and admired Goethe's novel *The Sorrows
of Young Werther* in translation. Goethe translated her *Essay on
Fiction* and said of *The Influence of the Passions on the Happiness of Individuals and of Nations* that he found in it "Most
beautiful thoughts, human and intellectual sympathies."[2]

When Goethe sent her a copy of his *Wilhelm Meister* in April,
1797, she still could not read German. She admired the book's
binding and began the study of the language under William
Humboldt, who aroused her enthusiasm for German literature.[3]
In 1799 she sent Goethe her book *Of Literature,* expressed her
admiration for *Werther* as a literary masterpiece, and told him
she was learning German.

Influence of Villers and Jacobi

Two other men who influenced her interest in Germany were
Charles Villers, publisher of a French newspaper in Hamburg,
a city crowded with *émigrés,* and F. H. Jacobi, who came to
Paris in 1801 and became a good friend of Mme de Staël. It was
from Villers' articles on German literature and thought that she
received her information on Germany for the book, *Of Literature.*
He was known as an exponent of the philosopher Kant. When
she decided finally to visit Germany, it was Jacobi who provided
her with introductions to German authors.

In the summer of 1803 Germaine was restlessly waiting in Coppet for permission to go to her beloved Paris. Napoleon's order of exile to a distance of twenty-five miles from the capital was in force. In September she and Mathieu de Montmorency, with two of her children, Gustave and little Albertine, arrived in Mafliers. The house she rented was uncomfortable for winter living, and she hoped to get permission to move to Paris. Unfortunately, Mme de Genlis, who hated her, sent false reports of her activities to Napoleon. The First Consul reacted by informing Germaine that he would have her escorted by gendarmes back to Coppet if she had not left by October 7.

Her friends appealed to Napoleon, and his brother, Joseph, even invited her to visit at his home at Morfontaine, but Napoleon was adamant. The order of exile remained in force. October 15, a gendarme, very polite and with literary interests, appeared in civilian clothes at Mafliers with Napoleon's order. Germaine was frightened. She made up her mind to go to Germany but hoped against hope for a reprieve. With the gendarme in attendance as she did final business affairs in Paris she waited in vain for Napoleon's answer to her appeals. She saw at last no other way out, and with Benjamin, Gustave, Albertine, and servants she finally departed.

In December, 1803, she arrived at Weimar. Of the effect she there produced we have a favorable account by Wieland's friend, Bottiger: "The most pleasing thing about her is that kindliness of hers, and that natural ingenuousness. She astonishes and charms by her absence of pretensions, by her effort to place others to their advantage, by her skill in understanding their interest, and adapting herself to the most delicate nuances of a foreign individuality."[4]

Germaine with Goethe and Schiller

She impressed Goethe and Schiller often to the point of irritation and fatigue. Schiller commented on her intellectual power: "Trying to explain everything, measure everything, she will not admit the obscurity or impenetrability of any subject, and whatever the torch of reason cannot illuminate does not exist for her."[5]

Goethe felt that she did not always listen to his ideas but stuck to her own opinions. This stubbornness on her part aroused his ill-humor to contradict her. She was undisturbed, but wrote of him: "Nothing upsets the power of his mind and even the difficulties (*inconvénients*) of his character, his moods, embarrassment, constraint, pass like clouds to the base of the mountain on which his genius is placed."[6]

Goethe disliked the idea of treating serious subjects of philosophy and literary criticism in social conversation. Mme de Staël, however, had been accustomed all her life to using conversation for the interchange of ideas on subjects of the highest order, science and metaphysics as well as problems of government. The electric stimulus of conversation brought out new ideas and concepts to her flashing thought. Goethe expressed his final verdict when her great work, *De l'Allemagne* (*Germany*), was published. "It was a powerful instrument which made the first breach in the Chinese wall of old prejudices, raised between us and France."[7]

Berlin and Wilhelm Schlegel

In March she visited the court in Berlin and formed a lasting friendship for the two brothers Schlegel. She persuaded Wilhelm Schlegel to return with her as tutor for her two boys, Auguste and Albert, and as teacher and literary adviser for herself.

Wilhelm Schlegel had a superior mind, learned, logical, and precise. By 1804 he had translated sixteen of Shakespeare's plays —no small literary accomplishment. He has been called "the pedant of romanticism." Like many others he soon fell in love with Germaine, but submitted to her will, and served her the rest of her life.

Germaine had a fear of growing old. She was now forty. Her early attachments had been to men fifteen or twenty years older than herself, such as Narbonne and Talleyrand. Now her tender attachments were with men much younger than herself. Could it be one way of denying age? There was the handsome young Genevan, Prosper de Barante; the Portuguese poet, Pedro de Souza in Italy; Maurice O'Donnell, the Austrian officer whom she knew in Vienna in 1807; and finally John de Rocca in 1811. The last love was no infatuation, but a deep and sincere affection despite the differences of age and intellectual background.

Death of Necker

While she was still in Germany she had news of her beloved father's illness. Before she could return, the news of his death, April 10, reached her. Her grief was uncontrollable and she became hysterical. Benjamin Constant and her friend Sismondi tried in vain to comfort her. This was the moment she had feared for twenty years. Her remorse was the greater as she thought of the moments he was dying while she danced in Berlin. Her love and devotion to her father are well expressed in her essay on Necker's life: "I counted on him to make good my mistakes. Nothing seemed beyond remedy as long as he lived: only since his death have I known what real terror is; only then did I lose the confidence of youth. . . . In his strength I found my strength, in his support my confidence. . . . Where is he now, my protecting genius?" Her belief in immortality sustained her. Some day they would meet.[8]

After the death of her beloved father, Germaine's health suffered. She was advised to go to the warm sun of Italy. Napoleon gave his permission and letters of introduction, delighted to have her away from France. For six months she enjoyed, observed, and analyzed what she experienced of the Italian personality. She was much feted by the Italian *literati*. The result of her trip was the novel *Corinne*, written after her return to Coppet, and published in 1807. Its success was instantaneous and universal. It appealed as a romance, as a faithful picture of the great monuments of Italy, and for the philosophic thoughts which it expressed. She had dared complete her book at Acosta, Mme de Castellane's home, thirty miles from Paris. She waited there for the news of the reception of her book. Napoleon's hostility, which she had hoped to soften, was unabated by her success. In it she made no mention of him, though so requested by Fouché, Napoleon's chief of police.[9]

Plot of Corinne

The novel *Corinne* presents as its hero Oswald, Lord Nevil, handsome, intelligent heir to a great Scottish name. He is in poor health, grieving over the death of his father. At the age of twenty-five he is disillusioned, tired of life. Doctors advise him to go south for his health, and he undertakes the journey to Italy. His melancholy is increased by his remorse for not heeding his father's wish for his marriage.

Lord Nevil, in his grief, shows on board ship such kindness to others, such forgetfulness of self that both passengers and crew crowd around him on landing to thank him. War necessitates his avoiding France for the journey to Italy. He goes by way of Germany and Switzerland. His only moments of pleasure are spent exploring the Tyrol on his horse, which has been brought from Scotland. The peasants clap their hands at the sight of his courage and dexterity as he boldly skirts the edge of the precipice.

At Innsbruck, where he stays in a banker's house, he meets the Count d'Erfeuil, a poor French emigrant who desires a companion for the trip to Rome. Oswald offers to accompany him, though "his reserve suffered greatly at the prospect of finding himself thus thrown on the society of a man he did not know."

At Ancona, where they stop, Lord Nevil saves the people of a Jewish ghetto and the House of Maniacs from a conflagration when the forces of prejudice refuse to unlock the gates or put out the hospital fire. Arriving in Rome Oswald awakes the next morning to hear bells ringing and the noise of cannon announcing a great celebration. Corinne, the famous Italian poetess, and *improvisatrice*, is to be crowned at the Capitol, in a ceremony that is reminiscent of Tasso and Petrarch. Despite his English reserve and prejudice against publicity for women, he goes to the ceremony.

Corinne

Corinne has beauty, talent, a lovely voice, and gracious presence. "Attired like Dominichino's Sibyl,"[10] she is surrounded by a band of white-robed maidens. The portrait of Mme de

Staël by the artist Mme Vigée-Lebrun portrays her thus. Despite the majesty of Corinne's appearance, there is about her the look of one imploring protection.

Corinne is praised for her talents and deep enthusiasm by the Roman Prince Castel Forti. From her intonation Oswald suspects something English in her background. His interest is aroused. As she descends the steps, her crown of myrtle falls which Oswald retrieves and she thanks him. Again the mysterious English accent.

D'Erfeuil arranges a meeting. Oswald is impressed but is already troubled with presentiments and fears. Corinne is attracted to Oswald and invites him to return. She decides to make him love Italy so much that he will remain, and as his guide she shows him the magnificent monuments of antiquity.

Oswald, grieving for his dead father, and remorseful for not having acceded to his father's wish that he marry a Lucy Edgermond, is lifted out of his melancholy by Corinne's attentions and eloquent personality. He falls in love with Corinne. From this point on Oswald devotes himself to her despite inner presentiments of future difficulties. As for Corinne, Oswald's elegance and nobility of manner and his English reserve contrast with the lively and flattering tributes of her Italian admirers and win her love. Even the rational realism of Castel Forti does not convince Corinne of the unhappy difference in background and customs of the Englishman and her own. Corinne offers to show him Rome. "Time and chance," she says to Oswald's infatuation, "will decide whether the impression of an hour shall last beyond its day. If our souls commune, our mutual affection will not be fugitive; be that as it may, let us admire together all that can elevate our minds, we shall thus at least secure some happy moments."[11]

It is certainly Germaine's voice which we hear as Corinne continues: "We flatter, we deceive ourselves; and the very enthusiasm of which we are susceptible, if it renders the enchantment more rapid, may also bring the reaction more promptly. . . . I suppose no woman of heart ever reached the age of twenty-six without having known the illusions of love; but if never to have been happy, never to have met an object worthy of her full affection is a claim on sympathy, I have a right to yours." A little later Corinne adds, "In toiling for celebrity I have ever wished that it might make me beloved."[12]

Travelogue

The stage is now set for the drama to unfold. Corinne shows Oswald the Pantheon which, she says, appears more vast than St. Peter's because of the great space between pillars and the lack of ornament which overcharges St. Peter's. She muses on the ignoble fate of modern Italy where past genius is so well rewarded and remembered. The trip continues to the Castel Sant' Angelo and on to St. Peter's. Corinne (Mme de Staël) eloquently portrays the magnificence of Michelangelo's architectural triumph and its effect on the sensitive heart.

"You must have noticed," she says to Oswald, "that the gothic churches of England and Germany have a far more gloomy character than this. Northern Catholicism has in it something mystic; ours speaks to the imagination by external objects. The sight of such a building is like a ceaseless, changeless melody, here awaiting to console all who seek it."[13]

Referring to the low caliber of Italian governments, she continues, "With such soul for the fine arts, may not our character one day equal our genius?"[14] The faithful travelogue continues with comments on the Italian character and on historical Rome. In fact, Mme de Staël's description and accounts of history could provide the modern tourist with an interesting background. Corinne and Oswald go to the Coliseum, "The loveliest ruin of Rome! It terminates the circle in which all the epochs of history seem collected for comparison. Those stones, now bereft of marble and gilding, once formed the arena in which the gladiators contended with ferocious beasts."[15]

When Oswald interposes his English moral attitude, which saw only "the luxury of rulers, the blood of slaves," Corinne replies with eloquence: "Do not let your principles of justice interfere with a contemplation like this. . . . The very degradation of the Roman is imposing; while mourning for liberty, they strewed the earth with wonders."[16]

Rome is in a state of misery and degradation, but suddenly one beholds "Some broken column, or half-effaced bas-relief which will remind you that there is in man an eternal power, a divine spark which he ought never to weary of fanning in his own breast and of reluming in those of others."[17] To Mme de Staël this is the divine spark of enthusiasm.

Premonitions

Even the eloquence of Corinne cannot convince Oswald, who mingles a moral sentiment with all that he sees and feels. Corinne becomes conscious of the possible shipwreck of her love. The arrival of Oswald's uncle, Mr. Edgermond, impresses this premonition all the deeper upon her. Oswald is about to ask her to marry him, when the mention of his uncle's name upsets Corinne. Oswald now senses that there are secrets in her past which may betray their love. They mutually vow to tell each other their secret past, and a journey to Naples is planned. Corinne has Oswald's ring and promise. In the meantime Corinne weaves into their rapturous love comments on Italian literature and art galleries.

The journey to Naples brings a description of a visit to Pompeii and Vesuvius, but, most important for the plot, it is here that Oswald and Corinne exchange the stories of their past.

Corinne is the daughter of Lord Edgermond and his first wife, an Italian. When she was ten her mother died, but Corinne remained with an aunt in Italy until she was fifteen. Her father had married again, this time choosing a provincial English-woman of rigid conventions. Corinne, in England, could not adapt herself to the strict, monotonous life. She was too lively to be suitable as the wife of Lord Edgermond's nephew, Oswald. Lucile, the half-sister, was preferred in the wishes of the old lord, Oswald's father.

On her father's death, Corinne fled to Italy to live on her considerable fortune, and in England she was deemed dead. In Rome she developed her talents and won fame and glory.

Oswald's story was of an adventure with a Frenchwoman who proved unworthy. His father's death recalled him to his senses, and he suffered remorse.

A complicated set of misunderstandings separates the two lovers. Oswald has to return to England. Corinne, who has his ring and his promise of faithful love, secretly follows him. Thus his letters to her are never received and are never answered. Corinne falls ill in England. Persuaded that she has forgotten him, he sees Lucile Edgermond again. She is a gentle, ladylike English girl, obedient to her rigid Northumberland mother. She falls in love with Oswald, and a wedding is in preparation. Corinne, now recovered from her illness, arrives secretly to witness this love of her half-sister. Sacrificing herself, she sends back the ring by a messenger to Oswald and returns to Italy and her tragic fate. Her gift of poetry is gone and life holds no longer any promise of happiness. Despite the fond friends about her, she no longer cares to live.

The final chapters bring Oswald, after fighting in wars in the West Indies, to Italy with his wife and little daughter. Through the child's friendship with Corinne, Lucile discovers Oswald's past. Corinne makes one last appearance; too weak to recite her own verses, she dies.

An example of her eloquent stanzas is here given. The first two she wrote in Italy, as she tried to remake her life after her abandonment by Oswald.

> Why tell me I could charm, if not for love?
> Why inspire confidence to make me prove
> But the more fearful anguish when it died?
> Will he in any other meet more mind
> Than was my own? A heart more true and kind?
> 'Tis not first love that must endure;
> It springs but from the dreams of youth
> But if with intellect mature
> We meet the mind long sought in vain
> Fancy is then subdued by truth
> And we have reason to complain.[18]

This is Corinne's bitter complaint, or rather Mme de Staël's. This last strophe comes from her sad swan song as Corinne is about to die.

> O thou, my God! Oh, thou wilt not reject
> The offering of the mind; for poetry,
> Its homage is religious, and the wings
> Of thought but serve to draw more near to Thee.

It is again Mme de Staël's voice that we hear in Corinne's chant.

Mme de Staël's Analysis of National Character

Mme de Staël draws interesting portraits of national character. The Count d'Erfeuil has the wit, lightness, and even frivolity of the French aristocrat. He has lost an immense fortune and flees from his country but displays unchanging gaiety despite his reverses. His superficiality is revealed in his attitude toward the ruins of Rome, "rubbish covered with briars." He declares that a rapture which must be purchased by study cannot be very vivid in itself.[19]

Her description of the cold, conventional English women of Northumberland, kept close in domestic family bonds, contrasts with the creative, enthusiastic, unconventional Corinne. In Mme Edgermond she may be portraying her repressive Calvinist mother. She speaks of the "domestic worth of English women who bloom in the shade," among whom "there were some not deficient in mind, though they concealed it as a superfluity, and toward forty this slight impulse of the brain was benumbed like all the rest."[20] We feel Mme de Staël's personal protest in justifying herself through Corinne.

She defends the Italians against Oswald's criticism of their infidelity and desire for dissipation. She finds them capable of bravery and passionate, although indolent. Above all they are kind, have little use for ridicule and treasure their happiness. They rank genius high and hold a superior woman in esteem. This is a slap at the French society in which Mme de Staël had suffered.

Oswald, Lord Nevil, is the English lord, sincere, reserved, melancholy, believing strongly in the conventional order of things. The conflict in his character between his passion and his beliefs make him swing back and forth, at one moment at Corinne's feet in adoration and later dominated by his sense of duty and cold reason.

Mme de Staël as Corinne

In her novel Mme de Staël reveals much of herself. Her tortured thoughts of death are reflected in Oswald's soliloquy. "There is such rapture in active life, in those violent exercises that make us feel the energy of existence! Then death may appear glorious; at least it is sudden and not preceded by decay; but that death which finds us without being bravely sought—that gloomy death which steals from you in a night all you hold dear, which mocks your regrets, repulses your embrace, and pitilessly opposes to your desire the eternal laws of time and nature—that death inspires a kind of contempt for human destiny, for the powerlessness of grief, and all the vain efforts that wreck themselves against necessity."[21]

The character and experience of Corinne translate Mme de Staël's own protest against the unhappy position of the superior woman in society. The eloquence and exuberance of expression of Corinne's passionate love and of her interpretation of Rome's antiquities belong to Mme de Staël. In fact, Corinne is actually an idealized and romanticized image of the author. If we compare the two novels, *Delphine* and *Corinne*, we find in both the same exuberant, romantic feeling as well as comments on national character and government, but whereas *Delphine* portrays eighteenth-century French aristocratic society, *Corinne* presents the foreign background of Italy and northern England. *Corinne* is of superior interest, although the plot is complicated. The theme of the superior woman abandoned by her conventional-minded lover is common to both.

Evaluation

The modern reader would tire of the artificial epistolary style of *Delphine*, but he would doubtless continue to read *Corinne*, his interest held by the poetic evocation of Rome and Italy and by the interplay of such contrasting characters as the two protagonists. Today's reader lives, however, in a totally different world; such impassioned characters and ardent dialogues as those of Oswald and Corinne would be difficult to find in twentieth-century literature. In 1807, however, both the melancholy, uncertain hero, and the tragic, passionate heroine were welcomed with enthusiasm. Sainte-Beuve[22] calls *Corinne* a "roman poem." He felt that in it she had corrected many of the faults of *Delphine*, that its style was consistent and firm and the conversations charming. A modern critic[23] disagrees, considering it "the worst great novel ever written," with a poor plot, and "hysterical and romantic in a ludicrous sense." He modifies this judgment by saying that *Corinne* is "the product of an extraordinary mind and temperament, lucid and chaotic in turns." As already mentioned in the discussion of *Delphine, Corinne* is another of the romantic novels with the poetic exuberance of expression and the passionate, ill-fated hero and heroine that reveal the "mal du siècle."

CHAPTER 10

Germany, De l'Allemagne

Coppet 1807-1810

THE CONSIDERATION of Mme de Staël's partly autobiographical novels leads back to her personal life during
these eventful years. The relation with Benjamin Constant,
begun in September, 1794, became an obsessive and possessive
bond of passion, which Germaine could not let go, nor could
Constant break it. They seemed to be necessary to each other,
though Benjamin, no longer in love, made many efforts to burst
these bonds and finally in 1808 contracted a secret marriage with
Charlotte von Hardenberg in his vain attempt. The scenes between them were stormy to the point of melodrama.

For several years Constant was like a captive bird on a string.
The story of his love affairs he made famous in the novel,
Adolphe, and in *Cecile.* His self-analysis was pitiless. It has
been said that Constant was the type of man who falls in love
with love rather than with the object of his desire.[1] His passion depended on "the tension of the pursuit, the intensity of
expectation," but once its object was attained he was overcome with lassitude and disillusion. He could not resist the
temptation to fall in love, but he was not heartless. His will
to escape from Mme de Staël was overcome by his tender pity.

The basis of the affinity between Mme de Staël and Constant was the intellectual stimulus which each had for the
other. Witnesses of their conversations tell of their electric
interchange of wit, ideas, and paradoxes which made the conversational exchange of others like the rumble "of farm carts
along a lane."[2] In contrast with the sterile years he spent with
Mme de la Charrière, Constant found in his relationship with
Germaine an awakening of confidence in himself, even to the
point of personal ambition in a cause. It was her influence which

[111]

encouraged his political writings and which had him named to the Tribune in 1800. He realized his great debt to her, though he chafed at her yoke. His realization of her devotion to him and his weak will held him, but did not prevent many betrayals and deceits by both. Albertine, whom he loved tenderly, was the child of their love. For fifteen years their relationship, though stormy, remained a close one.

The years 1804-10 were gay and brilliant at Coppet when Mme de Staël was in residence. Distinguished foreigners were entertained; Coppet became a center of political intrigue as well as a literary and dramatic workshop. It became as famous as Voltaire's "Ferney" as one of the intellectual centers of Europe.

Mme de Staël gathered her friends together, Juliette Récamier, Mathieu, Constant, and Wilhelm Schlegel, for dramatic representations. In the library was set up an excellent little stage with backdrops and professional properties. People came from nearby Lausanne and Geneva and even from as far as Berne to see these amateur actors present Racine and Voltaire. Mme de Staël loved to act in these dramas and possessed an excellent memory herself. Three of the plays, from the pen of Germaine herself, were *Géneviève de Brabant*, *Hagar in the Desert*, and *La Sunamite*, in which Mme de Staël appeared with her children. The high point of the dramatic representations was reached in the production of *Andromaque* in 1807, in which Benjamin played the part of Pyrrhus to Germaine's Hermione.

Mme de Staël and her many friends organized parties, discussions of all sorts, wrote plays, and produced some notable presentations of French classics in the lovely drawing room. Breakfast was at ten, the main meal at five in the afternoon, and supper was served at eleven. Madame de Staël characteristically went about the house carrying her green morocco writing pad. She wore elaborate turbans of emerald and scarlet, and bright-colored scarves to enhance her beautiful eyes, and to distract others from noticing her oatmeal complexion and thickening body. In her fingers she carried a sprig of laurel, myrtle, or willow, which she twirled or waved in the air as she talked.[3]

Her dominating personality and activity were a strain on those around her. She scolded, praised, interrupted, commanded, and sometimes frightened those around her by her moods of passion. Constant wrote in his diary, "If she knew how to rule herself, she could rule the world." She wearied her guests by her incessant activity. Fanny Randall, Albertine's English governess, was a rock of calm in the whirling emotions of life at Coppet. It was Fanny who devotedly nursed Mme de Staël in her last illness.

During all this activity Mme de Staël did not stop writing. She wrote even while her hair was being dressed. Her correspondence with friends and acquaintances, and European notables, was prodigious. She wrote to President Jefferson in 1807 of the possibility of her son's emigrating to America.[4] In 1812 she wrote again to him in an attempt to make peace between England and the United States.

It was in 1807 that her notes on Germany gave her the impulse for further study, and a new book took shape in her mind. She would reveal Germany to the French. She began writing *De l'Allemagne*. It was for more information, as well as to escape from Coppet exile, that she made a second trip to Germany and to Vienna.

The Vienna she visited had changed from the one she knew on her previous visit, from the eighteenth-century spirit of toleration to one of snobbery and derision. It laughed at her eccentric décolleté clothing, which bared her fleshy arms and shoulders.[5] It also laughed at Beethoven's music. She spent five months in Vienna, where despite her faults of etiquette she was entertained in all the aristocratic houses. The great music of the day, Beethoven's, Haydn's, Mozart's, and Gluck's she heard and appreciated, but she did not wax enthusiastic in her writings.

In Vienna she again indulged her love of acting and put on private theatricals of which Marivaux's *Legacy* and Molière's *Les Femmes Savantes* were successful. She organized a series of public literary lectures on Elizabethan and Spanish drama which Wilhelm Schlegel gave for the fashionable public, lectures which are still worth consulting today. These lectures were well received and distracted Schlegel from his jealousy at her affair with the Austrian O'Donnell.

In May she began her journey back to Coppet with a triumphant return by way of Weimar and Dresden. It was in the fall of 1808 that Mme de Staël became interested in German mysticism along with her circle at Coppet. There had come to Geneva a Mme de Krüdener, a converted mystic who preached God's love. She had written her confessions in a successful novel, *Valérie*, in 1803, a novel beside which Germaine's *Delphine* seemed almost tame. A year later Julie de Krüdener had had a sudden conversion from the dizzy social life in Paris which this novel had brought to her. Returned home to Riga she spent two years in good works and prayer and then traveled through Germany under the influence of various mystics until finally in 1808 she arrived in Geneva and was invited like many other celebrated characters to Coppet. Madame de Krüdener urged Germaine, who was suffering a period of depression, to relax in the quiet meditation of divine love, but this was beyond the power of Germaine, and Mme de Krüdener left Coppet with the remark, "We must leave Madame de Staël to God; she will not be able to escape Him."[6]

After the visit of Julie de Krüdener there came to Coppet another strange mystic, the wild, emotional evangelist, Zacharias Werner. It has been said that he united in himself all the Romantic strivings to an extreme degree. The combination of his excesses of sensual passion and sexuality with moments of mystical exaltation made him an unhealthy personality close to madness, although his writings had bursts of true poetry at times. His wanderings finally brought Werner to Switzerland where he met Mme de Staël and was eventually invited to her chateau. The discussions held by the chateau's odd assortment of guests, Schlegel, Oehlenschläger, Benjamin, Sismondi, Bonstetten and others dealt with literary productions but often with metaphysical theories of divine and earthly love. The best judgment of Werner was given by Sismondi when he wrote that Werner was "completely mad, though talented and kind."

Life at Chaumont

By the spring of 1810 Mme de Staël had nearly finished writing her book on Germany. She had spent six years in research and study for it, and two years composing it. She declared her intention of going to America and obtained passports, but she stopped near Blois with her manuscript to see the printer who had published *Corinne*. She rented the beautiful castle of Chaumont-sur-Loire, which had been at one time the home of such famous people as Diane de Poitiers, Catherine de Medici, and Nostradamus. It was about ninety miles from Paris. Here she assembled her children and an array of friends including her two best friends, Juliette Récamier and Mathieu de Montmorency. From this new home she could supervise the printer, and there were happy times before the storm broke, times of music, which she loved, and of playful amusement and writing. Her daughter Albertine accompanied on the harp Juliette Récamier's sweet voice.

Mme de Staël had first met the lovely Juliette in Paris in 1798, when her husband was purchasing a Necker property. Juliette was twenty-six, Germaine thirty-two. A close and tender friendship developed between the two women who were so opposite in character, the one impetuous and passionate, the other calm, virginal, and feminine. Constant spoke of the rapid fire of Germaine's ideas, and of the rapid comprehension of Juliette, which brought them together in mutual appreciation as long as Germaine lived. It was at Germaine's home in Paris that Juliette and Chateaubriand met. After her death they made the pilgrimage to Coppet together in memory of their friend.

By September 23 the last proofs of *Germany* were corrected. The censors had passed her book with certain changes, which she had made. This was in accordance with the new regulation concerning the printing of literary works. At the end of the regulation was a litle article which provided that even after the censors had passed a work, the Minister of the Police had the right to suppress it altogether if he felt it proper to do so. Mme de Staël, in commenting in her preface on this says, "A law was not necessary to decree what was in fact the absence of all law; it would have been better to have relied simply upon the exercise of absolute power."

Five thousand copies had been printed (2 vols.), and all seemed to be going well. Mme de Staël and Mathieu left for an excursion to Mathieu's chateau nearby. While she was gone, the order came from Napoleon's Chief of Police, Savary, the Duke of Rovigo, to destroy not only the printed copies, but even the plates and to confiscate her manuscript. She was to be exiled from France and was ordered to leave within three days.

Through her son's quick action a copy of the manuscript was saved. The five thousand printed copies were hacked to pieces. Three years later, in London, *Germany* was published, and it was well received. To her letter of protest against the illegal seizure and destruction of her book after passage by the censors, Rovigo replied, "It has seemed to me that the air of this country did not agree at all with you, and we are not yet reduced to seek for models in the nations whom you admire. Your last work is not at all French."[7]

She protested her love for France, remarking that such a love does not necessarily preclude her admiration for England. She destined her book to raise the glory of the works of the human spirit in French eyes.

It is true that in her enthusiasm to revitalize the French, she wrote glowingly of the Germans; she idealized them. For this she has been criticized.[8]

She did not approve *in toto* of the Germans, however. They lacked good taste and conversational excellence. They were too contemplative, too indifferent to politics; too slow and too stubborn; the military class was too dominant; the lower class too crude. She praised their industry, their power of intellect, their imagination as thinkers and writers but was shocked by their lack of independence of action in government.

Today three of Mme de Staël's books, *Germany*, *Literature Considered in Its Relations to Social Institutions*, and *Considerations on the Principal Events of the French Revolution*, remain of very significant interest. The ideas she interpreted have been incorporated into much of the world's thought since her day, thus emphasizing the importance of her intellectual role.

General Divisions of Germany

Mme de Staël divides *Germany* into four parts after the "General Observations." The first part is a study of the physical aspects, customs, and character of the Germans, as well as of the influence of chivalry and Christianity on the German people. Other chapters treat of Vienna, of different states of Germany, such as Saxony, Weimar, Prussia, and also of Berlin, where she was highly acclaimed on her visit in 1804. Education and its institutions, the German language, and the power of conversation come under her keen observation.

Part II treats of the arts and literature in Germany, of French and English attitudes toward them, and discusses German authors, Lessing, Goethe, Schiller, and others. She comments in separate chapters on individual literary works such as *Faust*, *William Tell*, and other works of Goethe and Schiller. Part II ends with observations on the novel, on German historians, on the critics August Wilhelm and Friedrich Schlegel, and on German fine arts.

Part III studies philosophy and morality and contains a comparison of English, French, and German philosophy. Two chapters are devoted to Kant and the philosophers before and after his time.

Part IV discusses religion and enthusiasm and includes chapters on Protestantism, the Moravian Brothers, Catholicism, and even the mystics.

In all these subjects Mme de Staël revealed, not only the working of her brilliant mind, but also the influence of her affections. Her judgments of authors were sometimes faulty and too personal, but her purpose—to inspire French thought to fresh new patterns—remained the central theme, glorifying her work for the Romanticists appearing on the horizon. She stood on the threshold of the nineteenth century. She revealed the Germans not only to the French, but to the Germans themselves.

In her "General Observations" she distinguishes three main races as forefathers of the principal nations of Europe—the Latin, the German or Teutonic, and the Slavonic. Climate, governments, and individual national history are factors to be considered in the character of each group. Ecclesiastical power has affected Italy; the wars with the Arabs have given Spain military spirit, but in general the Latin nations showed the character of a long-enduring pagan (Roman) civilization. The Germanic nations were civilized by Christianity, and their history is that of chivalry and "the spirit of the middle ages,"[9] Gothic rather than Classical. The civilization of the Slavonic tribes arrives much later and contains more imitation than originality. They borrowed from the French, and their Asiatic qualities are not developed enough yet to give their writers true and natural character.

The great difference between the French and the Germans lies in the fact that the French consider external objects as the sources of all ideas; and the Germans consider ideas the source of all impressions.

It is possible here to discuss only the main features of this monumental work, *Germany*. Mme de Staël again brings out her division of literature into that of the northern genius, imaginative, melancholy, dreaming, and Christian, and that of the south, the Greek and Latin, brilliant, colorful, pagan, sensuous, and happy. She contrasts the German character, sincere, faithful, serious, and dreamy, with the Latin character, gay, irresponsible, elegant, and witty. The Germans seemed to her to have qualities of imagination and of moral stability, to love music and the peaceful comfort of their stoves, beer, and tobacco. They are independent of rules in literature but in life prefer a well-marked line of conduct.

The French are feared for their use of ridicule. In French conversation "subjects are played with like a ball, which in its turn comes back to the hand of the thrower."[10] "A Frenchman can speak even without ideas; a German has always more in his head than he is able to express." "A German, unless he thinks, can say nothing." "When he has nothing to say, he smokes."[11]

She thought the Germans more original and independent in spirit than the French, who follow like sheep in fear of censure and ridicule.[12] Both nations, however, could learn from each other.

Ideas on Education

Discussing education, she rejected learning through amusement. "The mind of the child should accustom itself to the efforts of study, as our soul accustoms itself to suffering. . . . You may teach a child a number of things with pictures and cards, but you will not teach him to learn, and the habit of amusing himself, which you direct to the acquirement of knowledge will soon take another direction when the child is no longer under your guidance."[13]

In her "General Observations" she places the passage deleted by the French censor, "We need not, I imagine, wish to encircle the frontiers of literary France with the great wall of China, to prevent all exterior ideas from penetrating within."[14] Even if another literature seems lacking in good taste, it may contain ideas to enrich French thought, just as Racine's plays receive inspiration from the Greek literature, and Voltaire's tragedies from Shakespeare.

Her plea for independent thought and judgment is strong: "Opinions, which differ from the ruling spirit . . . always scandalize the vulgar; study and examination can alone confer that liberality of judgment, without which it is impossible to acquire new lights or even to preserve those we have; for we submit ourselves to certain received ideas, not as to truths, but as to power; and it is thus that human reason habituates itself to servitude, even in the field of literature and philosophy."[15] This servitude, of course, results in sterility. Here is her protest against conformity to set rules.

Chapter II, Part I, on the "Esprit de la Conversation" characterizes the French of Mme de Staël's day. Paris is the city known for its wit and its taste for conversation, but all classes of people in France feel the need to converse. Conversation for them is not just a means of communicating ideas, feelings, and transactions, "It is an instrument on which they are fond of playing, and which animates the spirits, like music among some people, and strong liquors in others."[16] She dwells on the delight which good conversation brings, its "electric spark."

This capacity the Germans lack; in this the French excel. She reveals here her own delight in brilliant conversation, a conversation which was a sort of bombshell to the sober Germans of Weimar. She continues: "The course of ideas for the last century has been entirely directed by conversation. Men thought for the purpose of speaking, and spoke for the purpose of being applauded, and whatever could not be said seemed to be something superfluous in the soul. The desire of pleasing is a very agreeable disposition; yet it differs much from the necessity of being beloved; the desire of pleasing renders us dependent on opinion, the necessity of being beloved sets us free from it. . . ."[17]

"German is better for poetry," she wrote, "French for prose." The fact that the meaning of a German sentence is not complete before the end is a handicap in conversation. French can express a thousand observations or turns of expression impossible in German.[18]

Languages and Learning

In foreign languages the problem is both grammatical and intellectual. "The child at first understands only the words, then he ascends to the conception of the phrase, and soon after to the charm of the expression, its force, its harmony . . . he introduces himself to ideas in succession, compares and combines different sorts of analogies and probabilities; and the spontaneous activity of the mind, that alone which develops the faculty of thinking, is in a lively manner excited by this study."[19]

She considers methods of teaching, that of Pestalozzi and of Rousseau, both in some detail. She agrees with Rousseau that the usual method of repetition without understanding is wrong, but "the remedy which he proposes is still worse than the evil."[20] "A child who, according to Rousseau's system should have learned nothing until he was twelve years old, would have lost six of the most valuable years of his life; his intellectual organs would never acquire that flexibility which early infancy alone could give them."[21] He would have acquired habits of idleness also. Rousseau's tutorial method would require every man to devote his whole life to educating another being. Pestalozzi's method, simplifying the material, lets the child discover the material by himself.

Mme de Staël believed thoroughly in the value of the study of foreign languages, ancient and modern. "It broadens a man's thought beyond that of his own nation." "Besides," she wrote, "the study of foreign languages requires the same discipline of attention as mathematics. Grammar unites ideas as calculation combines figures."[22] She devotes a chapter each to Saxony, the birthplace of Protestantism; to Weimar, the literary metropolis, "The Athens of Germany"; to Prussia, which leads her to a study of Frederick of Prussia; and to Berlin, which has the faults of newness and of male domination.

Part II

Part II takes up the subject of German literature, historians, and fine arts. In literature she feels that the French are superior in style and dramatic art. Few French know German, and the beauty of German poetry cannot be translated in non-Teutonic languages. In German literature there are no set rules; a work is judged individually, and an author creates his own public.

Mme de Staël felt that the first condition for a writer was to feel strongly and vividly and to express himself with clarity. The Germans often took pleasure in being obscure. German talent was contemplative, worked in solitude, whereas the French worked in society.[23]

As she has done so many times before, Mme de Staël voices her admiration of the English, of their literature and their institutions. In Part II, chapter 2, she contrasts the English and the Germans. The English are pragmatic; they emphasize the useful, and their heads are filled with political considerations. Their philosophy is directed toward the welfare of human beings, not toward abstract truth for itself. This contrasts with the Germans who are shut out from political discussion and thus direct their philosophy toward new systems of thought, metaphysical abstractions. Among the German writers whom she praises and analyzes are Lessing, Wieland, Klopstock, Winckelmann, Goethe, and Schiller. Of Goethe she wrote that he could represent all German literature because he alone united all the elements which distinguish the German mind; his writing demonstrated a great depth of ideas, grace born of imagination, and a sometimes fantastic sensitivity.[24] "He is a man of universal mind, and impartial because universal;

for there is no indifference in his impartiality; his is a double existence, a double degree of strength, a double light which on all subjects enlightens at once both sides of the question."[25]

She praised Schiller for his genius and his integrity both as man and artist, "two inseparable qualities in a man of letters."[26] His writings were an expression of his great and good soul. "Schiller was the best of friends, the best of fathers, the best of husbands; no quality was wanting to complete that gentle and peaceful character which was animated by the fire of genius alone; the love of liberty, respect for the female sex, enthusiasm for the fine arts, adoration of the Divinity, inspired his mind."[27] "I vowed to him a friendship replete with admiration."[28]

With specific examples and specific analysis and at great length she revealed to her French audience the great qualities of the poetry of Schiller and the dramatic art of Goethe. This analysis included *Don Carlos, Wallenstein, Mary Stuart, Wilhelm Tell,* and the *Bride of Messina* by Schiller and *Goetz von Berlichingen, Egmont,* and *Faust* by Goethe.

Mme de Staël discusses style and versification in the German language. Of learning to pronounce a foreign language: "We listen to ourselves as if another were speaking; but nothing is so delicate, nothing so difficult to seize as accent." It takes a long succession of years, or the first impressions of childhood, to accomplish it. She felt that pronunciation was affected by diversity of climate and soil. This theory seems a bit far-fetched. "As we approach the seacoast we find the words become softer; the climate there is more temperate, but when we ascend towards the mountains the accent becomes stronger."[29]

She contrasts the German and French languages: "In French we say only what we mean to say; and we do not see wandering around our words those clouds of countless forms which surround the poetry of the northern languages, and awaken a crowd of recollections."[30]

Classic, Romantic

She took the word Classic to mean the poetry of the ancients, although it was often used to mean "perfect." The word Romantic she took to apply to the poetry related to the traditions of chivalry and Christianity; thus the division into literature before and after the coming of Christianity. In Classic art it was destiny which ruled. The base of man's actions was outside himself, in the gods. In Romantic art it is Providence which reigns, which the inner man questions, and which replies to him. Providence judges man according to his feelings and provides an intelligent order of things. The question to be considered in a literary work is this: Is it the work of imitation or of inspiration? The literature of the ancients is a transplantation; the literature of romance and chivalry is indigenous, national, blossoming under our religion and our institutions and in our modern nations. These are some of the ideas which the Romanticists were to illustrate in their future work.

Mme de Staël devotes several chapters to poetry. Men make use of images and metaphors when strong passion moves them. Common or primitive people express themselves poetically. Ariosto, La Fontaine, and Voltaire are society poets; Racine (in *Athalie*) is a lyric poet. Boileau improved French taste and language, but in so doing limited its poetic art. "In French we have masterpieces of versification."[31] However, the expression of prose subjects in lines of ten syllables is not poetry. Poetry is contained in our impressions of a beautiful landscape, a piece of music, the glance of a loved one, and above all in the religious feeling of the presence of the Divinity. The poet's gift is to reveal what lies deepest in his heart. Is not this what the romantic poets, Hugo, Lamartine, Vigny, and others express?

"Romantic literature is alone capable of further improvement, because, being rooted in our soil, it alone can continue to grow and acquire fresh life; it expresses our religion; it recalls our history; its origin is ancient although not of classical antiquity."[32] These words of hers spurred on the growing Romantic impulse of her times.

Of her chapters on German poetry and drama it is sufficient to note her admiration for the dramatic art of Schiller, and Goethe's art in composing elegies, ballads, and stanzas, often set to music. "The German poet comprehends nature not only as poet, but as a brother."[33]

Mme de Staël devotes one chapter to taste.[34] Taste teaches us what to avoid. It is a sense of the fitness of things, of propriety, not in the same way as in social relations, however. Taste in literature should allow some freedom for true sentiment and vigorous thought, or literature becomes stultified and lacks the creative spirit.

Dramatic Art

Chapters on dramatic art, and on the dramas of Schiller, Goethe, and Werner complete Part II of De l'Allemagne. What she had to say concerning these also influenced the Romantic school after her death. "A theatrical performance is literature in action,"[35] she wrote. "Of the three unities only one, that of action, is important." The others are subordinate. Foreign dramatists make theatrical illusion dependent not on the unities of time and place, but rather on characterization, on true observation of manners and the language of the period portrayed.

French dramatic technique, the unities, and the majestic Alexandrine do not fit the historical subjects of chivalry which she would have the drama develop.

She thought Shakespeare's dramas the greatest of all time. His tragedies and comedies were popular with all the English classes, whereas in France only the élite could really appreciate French tragedy; but Molière's comedies and the comic operas were enjoyed by all. Shakespeare's theater is sometimes so philosophical and profound that it needs often to be read even more than to be seen. If innovations are attempted in the French theater, the outcry is "Melodrama," but that is just what the people like and there is need for change. She does not denigrate the great French masterpieces, but pleads for innovation and for a greater resemblance "to that astonishing creature which is called Man."[36]

Here she repeats her purpose of exciting new ideas through what she shows of foreign literatures.

She has nine extensive chapters on drama, which include analyses of Lessing's, Schiller's, Goethe's and Werner's works. She analyzes with rare judgment the plays of each and points out their qualities in some detail, as well as their defects. She comments that German drama is more for reading than for representation, especially Goethe's works. She finds it unfortunate that there is no big city, no capital center in Germany for the creation of a good theater. Actors are found in one place; authors in another.

In the works of Goethe she finds tremendous variety of subjects and techniques. With Faust "he plunges himself into the stormy whirlwind of life."[37] In Mephisto he displays the bitterest pleasantry that contempt can inspire, and at the same time an audacious gaiety that amuses, "an infernal irony."[38] In the chapter on German comedy she quotes Wilhelm Schlegel's dictum that the ideal of tragic character is victory over our passions, that of comedy the power of physical over moral existence.[39] The Germans do not put into their comedy the ridicule of their own manners. They are too sensitive and do not handle pleasantry with lightness. She approves of the use of the ridiculous beside the tragic as Shakespeare has used it, because it heightens the effect of the pathos.[40] Both German and French Romanticists used this to great effect. In her previous *Literature* she had cautioned against this as a violation of good taste.

The Novel

Chapter 28 of Part II discusses the novel which, she says, has attracted more writers than any other genre, because it is the easiest. Its chief merit is to interest, to entertain, but there is danger in baring too much of the emotions of the human heart. *Werther* of Goethe, a passionate work of youth, is a masterpiece and portrays not only the sufferings of the heart but also the sicknesses of the imagination of our century. Is not this the origin of the later designation "le mal du siècle"? The morality of a novel consists in the sentiments it inspires. Of Goethe's *Wilhelm Meister* she writes that it is full of ingenious discussions; one could make of it a philosophical work of the first order if it were not mixed with the plot of a novel.

Historians

In Mme de Staël's chapters on German historians she states that since history is most closely related to the knowledge of public affairs, " a great historian is almost a statesman."[41] It is true that several of France's historians did take part in politics, for instance, Chateaubriand, Adolphe Thiers, and Guizot. She divides history into three groups, learned history, philosophical history, and classical history. The historians of antiquity were the greatest; the French are noted for *mémoires*. The Germans have many learned historians but their works are good only for consultation. Schiller leads the philosophical historians; he wrote history with feeling for patriotism and liberty, but the best German historian is Joachim de Müller. His *History of Switzerland* is a work of erudition and great talent; its author can be considered the true classical historian of Germany. She mentions Herder, whose writings included the subjects of theology and history. It is sufficient for our study to note how wide Mme de Staël's interest was and how clear, if not profound, her analysis.

Critics and Artists

Her chapter on the German critics, Friedrich and Wilhelm Schlegel whom she praises, sums up her judgment of the French and the Germans. By recourse to good French taste the vigorous exaggeration of the Germans is corrected, and the dogmatic frivolity of some Frenchmen is improved by the addition of the depth of German thought. "Criticism is not the narrow searching for defects, but the discovery of genius worthy of admiration."[42] Nations are so different in so many respects that not even a superior man can guess what the other nation is thinking. Hospitality to foreign ideas produces the good fortune of the one who receives them.

The final chapter of Part II focuses on the fine arts in Germany. Winckelmann's writings on the classical monuments of antiquity influenced all Europe to their study. Again she warns of the danger of imitation; the reproduction of sculpture in painting often led away from living nature. As in literature she urges the return to the inspiration of Christianity and of the Middle Ages as the source of modern genius, the new school. She mentions many of the painters and the musicians of Germany and she recognizes that the Germans excel in instrumental music.

Philosophy

Mme de Staël devoted all of Part III of *De l'Allemagne* to a consideration of English, French, and German philosophy and of ethics. She divides the study of German philosophy or metaphysics into three classes, one dealing with the mystery of creation, another with the formation of ideas in the human mind, and the third to "The exercise of our faculties without ascending to their source."[43] She feels that the first class, the study of the Creation, which the Greeks handled long before the Germans, leads only to the feeling of man's powerlessness and to discouragement. Mme de Staël is most interested in the second class, the formation of ideas in the human mind.

She believes that it is not probable that we can ever penetrate to the eternal truths which explain the existence of the world but that it is a noble task which leads us to examine ourselves and to ask whether our intelligence acts spontaneously or is excited by outside objects. Moral and religious questions depend on our answers. But there is a great diversity of systems between the French and German philosophers. She asserts that there are two ways of examining the metaphysics of the human mind: the first by theory; the second by the results of theory. The examination of the first she admits is beyond her capacity, but she can observe the influence of different metaphysical opinions on the development of the mind and soul; in other words, she can judge the philosophies by the works.

Do they serve the religious education of the heart, prepare us for an immortal destiny by the choice of good or evil? In her opinion the study of metaphysics should contribute to the moral perfectibility of man.[44] This study is dependent on logical reasoning as in mathematics, but its object is vague, in the clouds.

She observes that the origin of thought has occupied many philosophers. Are there two natures in man? If only one, is it the soul or the body? If there are two natures, do ideas come from the senses or are they born in the soul or are they a mixture of the action of outside objects on us and of our inner faculties?[45] This brings her to the question of free will or fate, which she traces in the works of the ancients and in the present thought. She emphasizes the importance for morality of the answer. What would conscience be if it were only the product of our senses, our habits, our environment?

English Philosophers

From this introduction she continues with a consideration of English philosophic thought, of Bacon, Milton, Locke, Hobbes, and several others. She examines and combats the materialistic or sensation basis of the philosophy of both Hobbes and Locke. Of Hobbes, according to whom all our ideas come from the impressions of the senses, she wrote: "He annihilates moral, as well as civil liberty; thinking without reason, that one depends on the other."[46] "He was an atheist and a slave . . . if there is in man but the impress of sensations received from without, earthly power is everything, and our soul and our destiny equally depend on it."

She attacks Locke for his theory that the consciousness of good and evil are not in man but are the result of experience. To prove it he relates all the countries where custom makes it a duty to kill one's enemy, to put to death one's old father, and so on. She argues that although the idea of just and unjust may be diverse, the conviction of the principle remains and this conviction is true of all human beings despite the diversity of circumstances. If, as nobody denies, the greater part of knowledge transmitted by the senses is liable to error, what sort of a moral being must that be who does not act until aroused by outward objects, and by objects even whose appearances are often deceitful?[47]

"A divine spark is the only indication in us of immortality. From what sensation does this arise? All our sensations fight against it, and yet it triumphs over them all . . . all that is truly beautiful in man springs from what he experiences within himself and spontaneously; every heroic action is inspired by moral liberty; the act of devoting ourselves to the divine will, that act which every sensation opposes, and which enthusiasm alone inspires, is so noble and so pure, that the angels themselves, virtuous as they are by nature, and without impediment might envy it in man."[48]

She introduces the chapter on the German philosophers with some general observations in which she again poses the theory of the divergent cultures of the north and of the south, the one influenced by Christianity, the other by paganism. She admits that her theory that the northern peoples were more speculative, the southern more practical, may have exceptions. The Greeks were speculative philosophers of a high order.

Descartes

The glory of Descartes is that of having directed the philosophy of his day toward the inner development of the soul. "I think, therefore; I exist; therefore I have a Creator, the perfect source of my imperfect faculties; everything without us may be called in question; truth is only in the mind, and the mind is the supreme judge of truth."[49] The writers of the eighteenth century studied chiefly political and social liberty; those of the seventeenth, moral liberty. The doctrines of materialism, with its contempt for all exalted sentiment, lead to immorality and are the origin of the licentious works of the late eighteenth century.[50] The spirit of frivolity reigns there. Voltaire's *Candide* is an example of this scoffing and "ferocious" philosophy.

German Philosophers

She discusses in separate chapters Leibnitz, Kant, Fichte, Lessing, and Schelling. Leibnitz is a man of great erudition, good faith, and an enthusiasm which he hides under forms and method. He treats the questions of the origin of good and evil and of man's inner sense of the divine. Mme de Staël reflects that, "if the mystery of the universe is above the reach of man, still the study of this mystery gives more expansion to the mind."[51] She concludes that we have to believe certain truths, just as we accept our own existence, because it is the soul which reveals them and reasonings are only "feeble streams derived from this fountain."[52]

Kant's *Critique of Pure Reason,* together with his *Critique of Judgment* influenced almost all that has been written in German literature and philosophy since its publication. Mme de Staël recognized the difficulty of sketching the principal ideas contained in them but admitted that there was no royal road to metaphysics. Kant, she said, "wished to re-establish primitive truths, the spontaneous activity in the soul, conscience in morals, and the ideal in arts."[53] Kant, in his *Critique of Judgment,* is especially remarkable. "He makes the sublime consist in the moral liberty of man struggling with his destiny, or with his nature." She humbly admits that she cannot in a few pages describe a system which "for twenty years has occupied all thinking heads in Germany."[54] "We must have a philosophy of belief, of enthusiasm, a philosophy which confirms by reason what sentiment reveals to us."[55]

What has here been related of Mme de Staël's analysis of the German metaphysicians is sufficient to prove her superior intellectual powers of understanding and analysis despite some contradictions and inconsistencies.

An amusing story is told of the first meeting of Mme de Staël with Fichte, whose system of philosophy was difficult to understand. "Can you give me, Monsieur, in the least possible time, for example, in a quarter of an hour, a rapid glance at your sys-

tem; what you understand by your 'moi'? I do not see it clearly."
Fichte did so. In a few moments Mme de Staël interrupted him.
"That is sufficient, sir. I understand. You work your system like
the Baron von Munchhausen who, arriving at a river with no
means of crossing it, seized his left sleeve with his right hand
and swung himself to the other shore."

Chapter 11 treats of the influence of the new philosophy on the
character of the Germans. She is disappointed that a philosophy
of the will, which should fortify character, seems to have little
leavening effect. The Germans are honest and upright as fathers,
private citizens, and administrators, but they bow before power.
They have little military spirit and are weak as a nation because
they are divided into small states, each different. They lack
energy, are heavy and crude, and hide their roughness under a
servile smile. Little did she realize that already patriotic forces of
revolt against the foreign invader and despotism were rising in
Germany. By the time *De l'Allemagne* was published in London
in 1813 German patriotism had been awakened from its idyllic
dreams. She herself had become the symbol of liberty to all
Europe. It is ironic that the nation which she was so enthusi-
astically describing would one day invade France not once but
three times in a century.

Ethics

In Mme de Staël's discussion of ethics, we hear her protest
against self-interest as the criterion of action: ". . . What would
become of the human race if ethics were nothing but an old
wife's tale, invented to console the weak, until they became
stronger? How should it be honored in the private relations of
life, if the government upon which all turn their eyes, is allowed
to dispense with it."[56] In the bloody Terror of the Revolution
the Communes of Paris set up the Committee of Public Safety
to assert that the supreme law was the safety of the people. But,
says Mme de Staël, "The only supreme law is the law of justice."
If morality is based on the careful calculation of self-interest,
there would be only clever or stupid combinations of a man's

conduct. A man's actions are moral only when dictated by duty and not determined by the fear of consequences. Governments are individuals which sacrifice their personal interests to the public good. "To permit ourselves the use of evil means even for an end which we believe to be good is a singularly vicious rule of conduct." We cannot help but feel that this entire discussion is directed at the government of Napoleon.

The chapter on "Love in Marriage" contains Mme de Staël's ideas on the relations of men to women. She asks why the holy union is so often profaned, and answers, "the cause is that remarkable inequality, which the option of society establishes, between the duties of the two parties." She was no militant leader for the enfranchisement of women. She did not plead for rights in political and civil affairs nor would she set up women as rivals to men. However, if women's destiny was devotion to conjugal love, then men who were the object of that love should have the same obligation.[57] In religion no difference is made in the duties of man and wife, but the world of society gives man the right of infidelity. Her protest is eloquent. Until this double standard is abolished, "there will always be war between the two sexes; secret, cunning, perfidious war; and the morals of both will suffer by it."[58] "Purity of mind and conduct is the first glory of a woman." Thus Mme de Staël turns the light of her reason on the external social question but leaves the example of her own life out of the discussion.

Part IV: Religion and Enthusiasm

De l'Allemagne begins and ends with the subject so dear to her heart, enthusiasm. To her and to the German writers it is the feeling of the infinite inspired by religious ideas. All our best and deepest feelings are penetrated with religion. Her prose becomes eloquent. "How sublime is that worship which gives us a foretaste of celestial happiness in the inspiration of genius, as in the most obscure of virtues, in the tenderest affections as in the severest of pains, in the tempest as in the fairest skies, in the flower as in the oak, in everything except calculation, except the deadly chill of selfishness. How beautiful is that religion which consecrates the whole world to its author. Religion is nothing if it is not all, if life is not filled with it."[59] We may judge from this that to Mme de Staël religion and enthusiasm as she understands them are closely related.

The chapters that follow deal with various religions and religious forms, the Protestant, the Catholic, the mystic, theosophy, and that of the Moravian Brothers. What characterized the Protestant leaders in Germany was the union of a living faith with the spirit of inquiry. Luther's convictions were stubborn, courageous, and fanatically inspired. The spirit of inquiry which the Reformation introduced made some people skeptics, others more firm in their religious convictions. Luther's great merit was that he placed the Bible in the hands of everyone and induced people to think about their religion.[60] This was progress, of which the human race is capable through education, but in France this perfectibility is often under attack. In the noble pursuit of truth religion has nothing to fear except from ignorance and secrecy. Her liberal thought cries: "Open the doors of the temple; call to your aid genius, the fine arts, the sciences, philosophy; unite them in one home to honor and understand the author of creation."

The Bible and its sources became in Germany the object of learned study and of prosaic theological explanation. It was Herder who first brought about a rebirth of faith through poetry. Catholicism in Germany was sincere and charitable; but it was a set established religion which did not accept examination. It was the Reformation which favored the entrance of new ideas.

Of the mystics Mme de Staël says that their religion is only a more intimate way of feeling and interpreting Christianity. It concentrates on spiritual love, on an inner peace, on resignation to the will of God. Fénélon and Lavater were examples of this religion.

In her chapter on "Suffering" (*Douleur*) she presents a curious imaginary conversation of two men[61] to console J. J. Rousseau, who thought himself the object of hate, envy, and persecution. The first man is an intelligent man of the world; the second is a religious recluse. Here is the gist of the arguments. The man of the world reasons: "Don't exaggerate your own importance; use your philosophy, your ideas of morality and religion to support you. If you don't like being a celebrity, just stop writing and you'll soon be forgotten. The romantic exaltation of your Héloïse doesn't help in daily living. Reason will

and does. Give up the friends who deceive and don't regret it."
Mme de Staël comments that Rousseau would probably be
induced to throw himself into the river.

The religious recluse speaks: "I don't know much about the
world, my son, but I know you are one of the company of good
men who follow the example of Jesus Christ and Socrates in
forgiveness. Try to endure envy; your talent is worth all the
agony it costs you. Thank God for your gift but remain humble
and do not judge unjustly. You may have to endure the cup of
betrayal for your own excesses; do not rebel but love more and
pray, for then you will not be alone. Let resignation come into
your heart; you will have your friends in spirit as you will one
day see them." We feel this is Mme de Staël talking to herself,
conscious of the twofold nature of her being, reason, and sentiment which conflict and which she cannot reconcile.

The chapter "Contemplation of Nature" shows how far she
was from having a real feeling for nature. Nature held for her
only an intellectual relation. The changing seasons with death
and birth bring her a melancholy thought, lightened by the hope
of resurrection. The ruins of architecture only inspire her to a
reconstruction of the past glory.

Enthusiasm

Already in the chapter on the influence of the spirit of chivalry
she observed that, "In all the great epochs of history, men have
embraced some sort of sentiment, as a universal principle of
action."[62] "The earliest heroes purposed the civilization of the
earth." Then came the enthusiasm of patriotism in Greece and
Rome, succeeded by the enthusiasm of chivalry in the Middle
Ages. This chivalry, born in the north, spread to the south, and
was evidenced in the poetry of love. The Crusades were a
manifestation of it. The last and fourth period of enthusiasm
was that of the love of liberty, originating in the epoch of the
Reformation. When it was replaced by the spirit of ridicule
and artificiality, a nation suffered and its women were ill-treated.

The last chapters of *Germany* explain her basic credo, enthusiasm. Enthusiasm to Germaine is the love of the beautiful,
the elevation of the soul to sacrifice; it is not to be confused

with fanaticism. "Enthusiasm is to the conscience what honor is to duty."[63] The Greek word for "enthusiasm" means "God in us." So to her it is the divine spark; it confers the greatest happiness. "It is the torch by the light of which we may understand countries, customs, and feel nature, perceiving under the veil of different sights the shadow of the Creator."[64]

Enthusiasm alone can counterbalance the universal tendency to selfishness, for enthusiasm means loving with heart and mind. It is destroyed by irony and ridicule. "Of all the feelings of the heart, enthusiasm confers the greatest happiness . . . indeed, it alone confers real happiness; it alone can enable us to bear the lot of mortality in every situation in which fortune has the power to place us."[65] Without it we are sentenced to mediocrity, monotony, and dullness of ideas.

"Writers without enthusiasm know of literature only criticism, rivalries and jealousies."[66] Enthusiasm which inspired her own writings brought her consolation for her suffering of exile. It made her impatient with mediocre minds but directed her to the intelligent thinkers of all nations and epochs. She had an amazing correspondence with men of letters and political leaders of the old world and the new.

Enthusiasm to Mme de Staël was the vital spark which redeemed all suffering and misery. Even in death it will not abandon us but remind us that the heart is imperishable, that "Our last sigh shall be a high and generous thought re-ascending to that heaven from which it had its birth."[67]

Mme de Staël ended *Germany* with an apostrophe to France in a passage that aroused the greatest hostility of the police toward the book:

O France! land of glory and love! If one day enthusiasm should be extinguished on your soil, if calculation should govern everything, and cold reason alone inspire even contempt for danger, of what use will be your beautiful skies, your brilliant minds, your fertile character? An agile brain, a skilfully managed impetuosity, might make you master of the world but the only trace you should leave on it would be torrents of sand, as terrible as the waves and as barren as the desert.

De l'Allemagne has been called "A political treatise."[68] As a condemnation of Napoleon's wars of conquest, of the subjection of one people by another, it was such a treatise. But it is much more than that; it is the result of a great and enthusiastic purpose to stimulate a nation to fresh creativity. It is the rich fruit of six years of research and thought by an exceptional mind and heart. Many of Mme de Staël's interpretations of her world of ideas carry inspiration for the world of the twentieth century.

CHAPTER 11

The Prison of Exile—
John Rocca and Escape

IN LATE 1809, even before the cruel blow suffered in the destruction of her book *Germany* by Napoleon's orders, Mme de Staël thought of leaving France in the summer of 1810 and going to America. She had holdings in New York State, and her friend Gouverneur Morris lived there.

Her friends warned her that she would not like materialistic America, but Germaine's head was filled with her vision of a new, generous, and independent country where she and her ideas would be well received. Early in 1810 she received passports for herself and son, Auguste, and in April she took the manuscript of *Germany* with her to France to her publisher, Nicolle, who already had in his hands the first chapters. After the destruction of her book in October, printed volumes, plates and all, it was too late in the year to make the Atlantic crossing. She returned to Coppet and strict police surveillance.

When the Empress Marie Louise gave birth to Napoleon's son, the future King of Rome, Mme de Staël was told by the Genevan prefect, Capelle, that if she would celebrate the event in a poem or eulogy, the persecutions would cease. Germaine refused, and when Capelle persisted in his request, she replied tartly that she wished the child a good wet nurse.[1]

New Life Despite Police Surveillance

From then on she was confined to Geneva, or a distance of five miles from Coppet. Her friends, Mathieu de Montmorency, and lovely Juliette Récamier dared to visit her at Coppet in spite of Napoleon's warning. As punishment both were exiled from Paris, to Mme de Staël's sorrow. Napoleon's police spied on her every movement. Despite this persecution she did not succumb to despair but instead she began to show a new interest in life. The reason for this new interest was that she had met a young French lieutenant of Hussars, of aristocratic family, handsome, passionate, and proud, a veteran of Napoleon's war in Spain. His wounds and broken health aroused her interest and maternal sympathy. John Rocca's father was a Calvinist and a distinguished citizen of Geneva. In spite of the great difference in age (he was twenty-three; she was forty-five), and in spite of her unlovely face and figure, John Rocca fell passionately and sincerely in love with Germaine. In her he found a woman's tenderness, which he had not known since his mother's early death.

The courtship was dramatic. Rocca rode his black Andalusian horse daily at a gallop in front of the house where she was staying in Geneva.[2] He performed feats of horsemanship before her windows.

He went to all the concerts and plays given at Germaine's house. He boasted to others that his love was so strong it would induce her to marry him. He became an object of public amusement, but nothing weakened John Rocca's perseverance. The strength and sincerity of his love finally won her consent to marriage. The wedding was kept secret, however, to protect her from the ridicule and criticism of her enemies, and to avoid his being recalled to active service. The ceremony took place May 1, 1811, with a Protestant pastor officiating, and Fanny Randall as witness. The public ceremony was performed much later, in 1816.

John Rocca

John Rocca was a gentle, loyal, courageous man; he was not articulate nor well read like Germaine, but his affection came at a time when she most needed it. Their frail son was born in greatest secrecy on April 7, 1812. His name was Louis Alphonse, but to Rocca he was "Little-Us." The baby was put in the care of Pastor Gleyre at the village of Longirod near Nyon. Not until 1814, on her return to France after Napoleon's defeat, could she claim the little boy who became so dear to Rocca's heart.

The Prison of Exile—John Rocca and Escape

Napoleon's spies surrounded Mme de Staël, ready to report everything she did or said, to Savary, the Duke of Rovigo, chief of police in Paris. Germaine's great fear increased that she would soon be imprisoned, "a fate more terrible than death to me."[3] She felt herself a plague to all around her. She sought comfort in prayer to God.

In a letter to her beloved Juliette Récamier, October 31, 1812, she wrote: "I do not think I will ever recover from what I am going through; nothing interests me any longer. . . . Life for me is like a ball at which the violin has ceased playing, and everything, except what has been taken from me seems colorless. . . . If I let myself give way I would present the most wretched spectacle. I have endless recourse to prayer, but it seems to me that I have wearied God, and that Heaven is deaf to me."[4] Even her faithful Schlegel was put under police ban, and exiled from Coppet.

Escape Planned

She began to project a way of escape. For this she needed to study the map of Europe.[5] To reach England was impossible on account of Napoleon's Continental System. Only Russia of the whole continent remained free of Napoleon's power and influence. Already the French armies were on the way to invade it. Her decision was to gain Sweden by way of Russia, a trip fraught with great danger and immense discomfort, especially for a woman just recovering from childbirth. Courage and determination, however, were not lacking in Mme de Staël, who never let her physical condition interfere with her course of action. Napoleon's power had to be opposed and defeated and her mind was made up to play her part in that defeat.

Her hope was to reach Russia, see Czar Alexander, arrange an understanding between Russia and Sweden, which were at war with each other, and encourage a coalition, which would include England, to fight Napoleon. Through agents during the previous years, she had already laid the groundwork of her purpose. Bernadotte, the French general whom she knew so well in Paris, was now Crown Prince of Sweden. She would be welcome in Russia and in Sweden as well.

In her *Ten Years of Exile* the story is told of her escape from

Coppet, and of her adventurous journey. She now had her loyal Rocca to accompany her and her young children Albertine (thirteen) and Albert (eighteen). There was no time to lose. Already Napoleon's armies were blocking off part of Russia.

Her Journey

She said goodbye to her cherished belongings, to the tomb of her parents, and to her desk, which had been her father's. She took his cloak to protect her in case the messenger of death approached.[6] One afternoon—it was May 23, 1812—she ordered her carriage as usual for a drive and told the servants she would be back for dinner. She had her fan in her lap, her children and Rocca beside her. In the men's pockets were the necessary articles for the trip. After driving a few miles she sent a servant to say they would return the next day. Instead of returning they traveled day and night to a farm near Berne, where Wilhelm Schlegel joined Germaine by secret agreement. Her son Auguste remained at home to take care of the affairs at Coppet.

The story of her evasion of Napoleon's police and agents on the trip reads like an exciting adventure. Her journey took her through Bavaria to Vienna, into Poland, Galicia and finally into Russia. It was July 14, the anniversary of French independence, and a day of happy augury for Germaine when she crossed the Russian frontier.[7] "Strange destiny for me," she wrote, "to flee first the French, among whom I was born, who carried my father in triumph, and to flee them to the confines of Asia."[8] She vowed never again to set foot on soil under the yoke of Napoleon.

One incident[9] is sufficient to describe the emotions of the trip. When she visited at Lanzut, Galicia, Prince Henri and Princess Lubomirska, who had sheltered French *émigrés,* she was frightened by the insistence of the police commissioner to accompany and watch her. It is here she had agreed to meet Rocca, and when she sees him riding to meet her, she motions him away for fear he will be arrested as a French soldier. She has an attack of nerves and is angry at herself when the policeman in pity sends for water to revive her.

The policeman insists he is supposed to sleep in her room, but he desists and Mme de Staël remarks she would have thrown him out the window had he forced the issue. Her reception by Prince Henri is most cordial.

Impressions of Russia

Mme de Staël's commentary on what she saw in Russia is interesting because some of her judgments, those of the Russian character, seem true to us today. She found the people friendly even to French-speaking strangers. The houses in Kiev looked like tents, which made the city from a distance resemble a camp, but there were some palaces and many churches with gold and green cupolas. The men were dressed in a blue tunic with a red belt; the women in bright colors. The country's monotony of the Ukraine plains was broken only by the rivers and ever present clumps of birch trees, and the land seemed to her "the image of infinite space."[10] There is so much space in Russia, she wrote, that the châteaux and the people are lost in it. The roads are rough and bumps send the couriers of the two-wheeled carts two feet into the air. Among the common people she found few comforts and no luxuries.

She was impressed by the Russian character, by the bigness of everything, the boldness, the unlimited imagination of the Russians. "With them everything is colossal rather than in proportion, audacious rather than deliberated upon, and if the aim is not always attained, it is because it is outrun."[11] "They are impetuous and reserved, more capable of passion than of friendship, more proud than delicate, more pious than virtuous, more brave than chivalrous, and so violent in their desires that nothing can stop them until they are satisfied."[12] She speaks of meeting a group of singing peasants, ignorant but free, hospitable and vigorous. Their vices belong to violence, not to corruption. "A Russian desire would blow up a city." The French would call them "barbares."

Poetry, eloquence, and literature are not yet well developed in Russia, she writes. When she views the great distance between the high and the low classes in Russia her impressions are colored by her opinion of the low estate of man under

Napoleon's rule. In Moscow she sees the rich giving their peasants in large numbers to the war effort and is moved by pity.

Mme de Staël was interested in everything, in the Kremlin, reminiscent of a Turkish mosque, the metallic sound of the Russian language, the gaiety and the melancholy of the peasants of the Ukraine, the Germans who filled the professors' posts at the university, the freeing of the peasants-turned-soldiers as their beards were cut, the St. Petersburg Museum with its skeleton of a mammoth, the tomb of Peter the Great, the country home of Catherine the Great.

At St. Petersburg she is glad to see the sea and the English flag. She has now "come back under the power of the Divinity." Her opinion of Czar Alexander is idealistic, influenced by the desires he expresses to her to better the condition of his peasants. One painful incident which she does not relate is that of a theater presentation of Racine's *Phèdre,* which was hissed and from which she was hustled away. Otherwise her reception in Russia was warm and gracious.

Bernadotte and the Czar Brought Together

Finally Bernadotte and the Czar were brought together to sign a treaty of mutual alliance. When the Czar's toast was drunk to the success of the English and Russian armies, she "felt bathed with tears. Must a foreign tyrant bring me so low as to desire that the French armies be vanquished?" It was Napoleon's defeat she desired, not that of France.

In late September Mme de Staël reached Sweden where a storm held the travelers on an island. Her story ends here and is never continued. Ill-health caused her to relinquish her story at this point, but she was soon to begin a new book, *Considerations on the Principal Events of the French Revolution.*

History has recorded the agony of the French army retreat from Moscow in October, 1812. Mme de Staël wondered if the loss of the army were not too high a price to pay for Napoleon's defeat. She was concerned about what would happen to France. Nevertheless, she organized a *salon* in Stockholm, where the diplomats met as they had at her home in Paris. Schlegel became secretary to Bernadotte, and her son, Albert, became one of his aides-de-camp.

It was largely through her efforts that negotiations began between the Allies to establish a new coalition army to defeat Napoleon. Swedish public opinion had to be swayed before Sweden would enter the group. Finally, Sweden and England signed a treaty whereby the Swedish army of 30,000 men would land in Pomerania. Prussia called up its army against Napoleon, and despite Napoleon's successes in May, Austria finally relinquished its alliance with France. The Coalition, established by June, 1813, of England, Sweden, Prussia, Russia, and Austria, assembled forces which even a Napoleon could not overcome. In October came his great defeat at Leipzig.

In the meantime after eight months Mme de Staël had enough of the rigors of Sweden's climate and the boredom of its society, and she traveled on to England.

Ten Years of Exile

Ten Years of Exile chronicles not only Mme de Staël's escape from France to Sweden and thence to England in 1812, but also her bitter struggle with Bonaparte. The book is in two parts. The first part takes Mme de Staël through her trip to Germany, her visit to Weimar and Berlin, to the beginning of the Empire of Napoleon and her opinions concerning it. At this point the narrative ends and is followed by her son's account of the five years which intervened between it and the second part of *Ten Years of Exile*. In it he mentions the publication in the autumn of 1804 of the work dealing with her father, his career and character, her trip to Italy for her health and the composition of her novel, *Corinne*, which she completed and published in France at the estate of M. de Castellane, some thirty miles from Paris. The publication of *Corinne* was such a success that Mme de Staël was again exiled to Coppet. There she began her work, *Germany*, which necessitated a trip to Vienna in 1807. Her return to Coppet the following year was the beginning of a brilliant social life at Coppet during which she wrote and presented her *Dramatic Essays* (mentioned in chapter 7) and worked on *Germany*, which took two years to complete. In the summer of 1810 she went to France and established herself and family group with Napoleon's permission within a hundred miles from Paris in order to supervise the publication of her work.

The second part of *Ten Years of Exile* begins at this point and describes in detail the circumstances of the destruction of her book and her return to intensified police surveillance at Coppet, from which she finally escapes to Russia. This portion of her narrative has already been discussed.

The account actually stops with her arrival in a storm at one of the islands in crossing from Finland to Sweden. Her son Auguste, the editor, adds that she arrived safely in Stockholm where she stayed eight months before continuing on to England.

The reason for writing this story of her years of exile, she wrote, was not to chronicle her own misfortunes, which were small in comparison with the public disasters, but rather to tell of "the great cause of threatened humanity."[13] She makes it plain that Napoleon's hostility toward her stemmed from her advocacy of liberty and independence of thought and action. She could not be purchased or bribed as so many of his followers had been.

Mme de Staël and Napoleon

I have already spoken of Mme de Staël's early enthusiasm for Napoleon which rapidly cooled as she saw him rise in unopposed power. He was declared First Consul for ten years, then Consul for life in 1802, Emperor in 1804 (May 18), and crowned and anointed by the Pope December 2. This period saw many military victories of Napoleon's armies, with intervening moments of peace. From 1804 to 1812 all of Europe was falling under the aegis of the imperial eagles, and Napoleon's ambition seemed to know no bounds.

Mme de Staël had bitter words for his advancement: "This first consul, designated the father of the nation which he was about to devour . . . this mixture of stupidity on one side (the people's) and cunning on the other: the stale hypocrisy of the courtiers throwing a veil over the arrogance of the master, all inspired me with an insurmountable disgust."[14] She saw his creation of a new nobility and the return to the pomp of the old *régime* as a ridiculous affair, one worthy of the pen of a Molière.[15]

She realized that Napoleon observed the weakness of each individual and played upon it for his purposes. He knew her love of Paris, and so made exile from it her punishment for not conforming to his will. As refuge against the suffering which exile caused her, there was the world of truths, the meditation of philosophy, and above all, her writings.

"From so many victories [Napoleonic] has one single form of happiness resulted?" she asked. The good administration which Napoleon organized in France was only in order for him to use France. Of the wholesale deportations without trial at the time of the bomb plot against Napoleon, she wrote in protest: "Every man is innocent until condemned by a legal tribunal."[16] She called the death of the Duke d'Enghien, the Bourbon prince, "murder cloaked with the mantle of law."[17] She protested against the treatment of the Santo Domingo King, Toussaint L'Ouverture, who was exiled to Switzerland and died there.

Napoleon himself felt the force of her hostility as she collected in her *salon* people of influence in his government. He remarked that people left her house less attached to him than when they arrived there. Since his effective weapon against her was exile from the Paris she loved, he used it with varying degrees of severity. For instance in 1803, when she thought he was too busy building flat boats at Boulogne to invade England for him to take notice of her, she ventured a few miles from Paris. Immediately a police chief from Versailles appeared, ordering her to a distance of forty leagues (100 miles), but allowed her to go to Paris to do business. In Paris she dawdled, and was hospitably received by Joseph Bonaparte and his wife, who often softened his brother's harshness. By 1812, however, Napoleon's order of strict exile had made Germaine's life unendurable. To reach England was her only way to reach security.

In England

The English court, including the Queen and Prince Regent, received her cordially in June. To the men of political influence in London she held forth eloquently, and was the center of attention. No writer on the Continent, except herself, had stood up in steady opposition to Napoleon, a fact which earned her general recognition. Byron expressed to her his views on *Delphine* and *Corinne*, saying he thought them dangerous material morally to put into the hands of young women, whereupon he enjoyed her impatient and angry protest. He commented that she should have been a man.

In October, 1813, she finally published *Germany* in London. It was a great success, selling out completely in three days.[18] News of the death of her impulsive, fiery son, Albert, in a duel in Hamburg with a Cossack soldier, and of the death of Narbonne, her former lover, saddened her but she kept up her courage outwardly, although she felt old and exhausted within.

The man who perhaps was most impressed by her was William Wilberforce, who influenced her to speak and write for the abolition of the slave trade. Her closest English friend was Sir James Mackintosh, who visited her almost every day, and aroused Rocca's jealousy. She was the object of many invitations, and she shocked the delicacy of the English matrons by her free, un-selfconscious manners. In his jealousy Rocca became difficult. He was not an educated man nor a man of intellectual interests, although Mme de Staël had tried to cultivate these in him. He could not see why she surrounded herself with so many admirers if she truly loved him so much. Germaine kept Rocca close to her heart, but needed the stimulus of other affections.

It was in October, 1813, that Napoleon received the disastrous setback at Leipzig, but it was not until April, 1814, that he was decisively defeated and made unconditionally to abdicate. The question had already come up as to who was to assume the leadership of France, Bernadotte, the crown prince of Sweden or a Bourbon prince, the brother of Louis XVI. Mme de Staël had secretly worked for Bernadotte to be the head of France instead of the Bourbon prince. The British, however, seemed to favor the latter. When Louis XVIII's representative called on Mme de Staël in November, requesting her to lend the power of her pen to the cause of the restoration she replied that she did not mix in politics.[19]

Benjamin Constant and Wilhelm Schlegel were also working for the cause of Bernadotte to replace Napoleon, the solution which Mme de Staël then favored; but Bernadotte hesitated as the Coalition Army entered France. He did not enter Paris with the Allies and forfeited his chance. Talleyrand's influence for the royalist restoration of the brother of Louis XVI was victorious in April. On this period, Guerard makes the following comment: "Alexander, Czar of Russia, promoted, but with no excessive eagerness, the candidacy of Bernadotte. It took the subtle machinations of Talleyrand and Fouché and a vigorous pamphlet by Chateaubriand, the recognized head of French literature, to make a Bourbon restoration appear as the inevitable solution."[20]

Early in 1814 one of the English ministers had asked Mme de Staël what she thought of the political situation in France. She replied, "I hope that Bonaparte will win and be killed."[21] She could not bear the thought of France being brought to bite the dust, neither could she wish for Napoleon's *régime* to continue. She opposed the memorandum sent her by Benjamin. "I'll do nothing against France," she wrote to him. "I will not use against her in her misfortune either the reputation I owe to her, or the name of my father who loved her. These burnt villages are on the very road where the women threw themselves on their knees to see him pass. You're no Frenchman, Benjamin."[22]

The Allies were finally victorious over the French armies, capturing the heights of Montmartre. Paris capitulated, and Napoleon was forced to abdicate unconditionally April 11, 1814. He was exiled to the island of Elba, off the coast of Italy. Madame de Staël did not join the wild rejoicing at his defeat. She was not vindictive, and she had no hatred for him in his fall. The Bourbon Restoration meant to her that the work and sacrifice of the Revolution of 1789 were erased.

Return to France

In May she returned to France, thin, pale, and nervously ill. The sight of the occupying soldiers in Prussian uniforms in Calais distressed her. Would she ever see the dawn of liberty in France? A month after her return she recognized that only the support of a stable government, Bourbon though it be, could rid France of foreign forces. She opened her *salon* in the Rue Royale and let her ideas be known. Her old friends returned —La Fayette, Mathieu, Juliette Récamier, Talleyrand, and Constant. Visitors to her *salon* were the Duke of Wellington, the two brothers Humboldt, Sir James Mackintosh, Bernadotte, and Prince Frederick of Prussia. Never had her *salon* been more influential.

For the summer she returned to Coppet with Rocca, who was now suffering from consumption. She, too, felt ill and again was taking opium to give her rest and ease the pain of her illness. However, she continued to work on *Considerations*. In the fall she returned to Paris with the definite purpose of regaining the two million francs of her father's loan to the nation for her daughter Albertine's dowry. She was now unpopular at court.[23] A letter to her old friend, Joseph Bonaparte, had been intercepted and read by Louis XVIII. Mme de Staël, however, never abandoned her old friends. Even Napoleon at Elba received her warning of an assassin's plot against him.

The Hundred Days

In March, 1815, came the news of Napoleon's escape from Elba and his return to power. Mme de Staël was sick and low in spirits, and she was afraid to remain in France. Napoleon, however, appeared to be a changed man. He told Benjamin Constant, his former opponent, who joined him, that he wanted a constitution for France, free elections, and liberty of the press. It was Constant who drew up the articles of this constitution. It has been said that Napoleon offered to be a more vigorous and more intelligent Louis XVIII. The constitution, or "Acte additionel" to the Constitutions of the Empire, as it was called, was ratified by a listless plebiscite. The nation did not rise to the support of Napoleon. His soldiers were no match for the massed troops of the Allies. The Battle of Waterloo, June 18, 1815, ended the Hundred Days, and Napoleon's imperial career. He was taken by the British to St. Helena, a lonely little island in the Atlantic, where he died six years later. Louis XVIII was returned to power.

Repayment of Necker's Loan to France and Albertine Married

During these months at Coppet Germaine was busy working on *Considerations* but her thought was also preoccupied by finances. Albertine had fallen in love with the young, but poor, Victor, Duc de Broglie, and a generous dowry was in order. Finally under Louis XVIII Mme de Staël's request for the repayment of Necker's loan of two million francs was granted. Auguste de Staël arrived with the good news in Italy, where Germaine and Albertine had taken Rocca for his health. With great joy she saw the happy marriage, the civil ceremony in Leghorn, February 16, 1816, and the double religious ceremony February 20 in Pisa. A great anxiety was removed from her mind.

Final Order Put in Her Affairs

Returning to Coppet for the summer of 1816, she was busy on the final draft of *Considerations*. She feared death and wished to put her affairs in order. Her marriage to John Rocca, or as she preferred it, John de Rocca, was publicly acknowledged. Her finances were carefully arranged, and her generous will was settled.

Her Salon Popular Again

She spent the autumn in Paris revising *Considerations* for publication. Its ideas, called the "creed of a lifetime,"[24] influenced the men who later overthrew the Bourbon dynasty. Germaine's *salon* and her teas and dinners were again popular. Her health, however, was at a low ebb, although she kept active through her will power and her intellectual vigor. In February, 1817, she was walking up the stairs to a reception, when she swayed and fell into the arms of her son-in-law. It was a stroke. For over three months she lay flat on her back, but improved and received friends with a lucid mind. In March she became a grandmother to Albertine's baby girl. Chateaubriand visited her, and there he met Juliette Récamier.

Chateaubriand's description of Mme de Staël comes from *Mémoires d'Outre-tombe*.[25]

She reclined, supported by pillows. I approached her, and at first I could hardly see the invalid. . . . Her quick glance recognized me in the darkness and she said, "Good day, my dear François. I am suffering, but not too much to love you still." She extended her hand, which

I pressed and kissed. On lifting my head I perceived at the other side of the bed a pale and wasted figure—it was M. de Rocca. He also was dying. . . . He did not speak, but bowed as he passed me—his steps could not be heard; he departed like a shadow. Pausing a moment at the door, he turned towards the bed, and, with a motion of the hand, took leave of Madame de Staël. The expiration of a great talent affects more than the dying individual; society is struck by a general disaster; each member of it suffers a loss. With Madame de Staël closed a momentous portion of my times. Her death made one of those breaches which the fall of a superior intellect produces once in an age, and which can never be closed.

Mme de Staël recovered enough to be able to make light of her illness and to enjoy her garden in a wheelchair. Her mystical faith in a God of Love and in immortality strengthened her to endure the difficult weeks bravely.[26] Albertine served in her mother's place at their dinners.

On July 13 she talked politics with the Duke of Orléans, and Mathieu visited her. Rocca was always by her side. Sleep never came easily to her, and opium relaxed her, so that night she had a small dose of it. When faithful Fanny Randall awoke by her side the morning of July 14, that glorious day of French Independence, she found Mme de Staël silent in death. Benjamin Constant and Victor de Broglie together watched over her that night. Her body was taken to Coppet and placed in the family chapel at the foot of her beloved father's tomb.

Benjamin Constant wrote: "Those who only feebly regret her loss will not know how to describe her, and those who regret her passing, as she deserves to be regretted, cannot find words."[27]

Considerations on the Principal Events of the French Revolution

Method and Purpose of Composition

CONSIDERATIONS on the Principal Events of the French Revolution was published by Mme de Staël's son, Auguste, and her son-in-law, Victor de Broglie, after her death. It is probably the most important of all her works because of its political ideas and influence. Her son's preface describes her method of composition. She traced the complete outline of the work, which she had conceived without referring back or interrupting the course of her thoughts, "except to make some research." Then she took this outline, transcribed it in her own hand, modified the expression of her ideas, and gave it to a secretary to copy. Then only did she make corrections of style, and she also made them in the printed galleys. She spent a year revising the first two volumes and part of the third. Many of the last chapters were not revised.

In her own Preface she explained that her purpose had originally been to examine only the political acts and writings of her father. That subject, however, led her to trace the events of the Revolution and to picture England and its political institutions as a justification of M. Necker's opinions.

Perfectibility of Mankind

Considerations expressed on its first page the conviction, which Mme de Staël carried throughout her life, that the course of history demonstrated the perfectibility of mankind; that the French Revolution was one step in that demonstration; that it would continue despite interruptions such as the excesses of the Terror, and the despotism of a Napoleon or a Bourbon. Her opening words were eloquent: "The Revolution of France is one of the great eras of the social order. Those who consider it the result of accidental causes, have reflected neither on the past nor on the future; they have mistaken the actors for the drama; and in seeking a solution agreeable to their prejudices, have attributed to the men of the day that which had been in the course of preparation for ages."[1] She hopes she can be impartial in her judgments. On the whole she was.

She makes the point that the Greek and Roman nations disappeared from the world as a result of their unjust institutions, among which was slavery. She sketches the different periods of history as she had done in her books, *Germany* and *Literature*, the feudal system (chivalry), then the beginning of enfranchisements and rise of the bourgeoisie, the period of despotism, and finally that of representative government. After examining the other European nations she decides that England "is the only great European Empire that has yet attained what, in our present state of political knowledge, appears the perfection of the social order.[2]" England had emerged from a period of fifty years of revolution—Charles I to William III—with a constitution, "the finest monument of justice and moral greatness existing in Europe."[3] When she is criticized for advocating that the French copy the English government system in certain respects, she replies that she doesn't see why the French or any nation should refuse to use the compass because it was the Italians who invented it.

French History through the Revolution

Chapter 2 traces French history as a struggle for liberty confirmed by law, from the time of the enfranchisement of towns through the reigns of the French kings. The subsequent chapters are devoted to an analysis of the circumstances and causes leading to the Revolution. For years little order had been established in the finances and postponement of the correction of long-standing abuses had been the rule. The King could not refuse financial grants and favors to courtiers, which raised the expenses even above those under Louis XV.

[152]

Of Louis XVI she writes: "An unfortunate fatality placed the reign of Louis XVI in an epoch in which great talents and great intelligence were necessary to struggle with the spirit of the age, or rather to make a reasonable pact with this spirit." Some of the aristocrats claim that a more decisive king could have prevented the Revolution, but in reality the claims of the people had become too strong under Louis XV. Her father, Necker, tried to introduce some measure of economy into the government and only made enemies at court. The adoption of his plans might possibly have averted the crisis by gradual and just reform.[4] His plans, however, were not supported by the King.

She devotes several chapters to the character of her father as a man of public affairs and to his management of the finances. She gives proof of his high moral character and honest conduct of his office. When the question comes up why the French people were so cruel in the Revolution she finds the cause in their "unhappiness," in their misery and ignorance and frustration which produced a spirit of desperation and a consequent lack of morality.[5] The dominance of the ignorant, fanatic, and hungry elements of the Paris communes had a large influence on the tragic course of events. The bankruptcy of the government, owing in part to the assistance given to the cause of the American Colonies, a cause dear to most Frenchmen, brought the downfall of the ministry and the recall of Necker. For seven years Necker had suffered in exile over his failure. When recalled he feared it was too late to restore the government. She described his triumphant re-entry into France with enthusiasm and her description of the events which followed was clear and unusually objective for a person who had lived through these events. They have already been related in Chapter 4.

She commented on the States General, "Yet there were symptoms of a certain arrogance of power among these sovereigns of a new kind, who considered themselves depositories of a power without limits, the power of the people. The English had proceeded slowly in forming a new political constitution; the French, seeing it had stood its ground firmly for more than a century, ought to have been satisfied with its imitation."[6] The Assembly, seized with enthusiasm for the American example, should have realized that what suited a new people could not be adapted to an old nation with its privileged caste.[7]

Chapter 3 is especially interesting to Americans, since it deals with General La Fayette and the French Bill of Rights, which he proposed to the Constitutional Assembly. He was a fervent Republican who, at nineteen, young and of a noble and affluent family, had left a wife and child to serve in the American Revolutionary cause across the sea. Madame de Staël likens his enthusiasm and opinions to those of General Washington.

Chapter 4 deals with the abuses of the *ancien régime* and relates the good effected by the Constitutional Assembly. Some of the wrongs and abuses which were abolished may be mentioned here: penal laws against the Protestants, who now had liberty of public worship; *lettres de cachet*; the hated *corvée*; secret criminal processes which were replaced by trial by jury; salt and tobacco taxes; and unequal taxation.

It is possible here only to outline her detailed account of the tragic events of the Revolution. Part I deals with the period to the fall of the Bastille in 1789. Part II carries through the March on Versailles, the confiscation of valuable Church property to fund the debt, the requirement of an Oath of Allegiance to the Constitution by the clergy, and the attempted flight of the King, June 21, 1791. The vivid description of the events in which she participated is found in chapters 4, 5, and 6.

In Part III she discusses the emigration and its tragic effect of depriving the nation of many of its best minds. There are vivid chapters describing and analyzing the course of events: the Anniversary in 1792 of the fall of the Bastille; the result of the Manifesto of the Duke of Brunswick; the bloody event of August 10, with its overthrow of the Monarchy (the King was confined to the Temple prison); the trial of Louis XVI; the Reign of Terror; and the fall of Robespierre. Part III ends with a description of the twenty months of the life of the Republic (November, 1795 to September 4, 1797), and the final arrival on the scene of General Bonaparte.

Certain of Mme de Staël's convictions are given here in her own words:

"To grant political rights without just reason to exercise them is an usurpation as much as any other."[8]

"The freedom of the press is the only right on which all the others depend and can be annulled only in case of foreign invasion."

[154]

"Nations have a sincere religion only when it is not related to politics and where the priests have no power in the state."

"Persecution in politics leads to nothing but the necessity of further persecution. . . . The object should be to extinguish hatreds and not to compress them."[9]

"Thomas Paine was the most violent of the American democrats," but "He alone advised what would have done honor to France, if it had been adopted, the offer to the King of asylum in America. The Americans are grateful to him, said Paine, for having promoted their independence."[10]

Discussing Napoleon's invasion of Switzerland, she makes the famous defense of her actions: "In every circumstance of my life the errors which I have committed in politics have proceeded from the idea that men were always capable of being moved by the truth, if it was presented to them with force."[11]

Rise of Napoleon

The first volume of *Considerations* ends with a description of the establishment of the Republic and a government by a Directory. The second volume is devoted to the rise of Napoleon through the faults committed by those in power. Mme de Staël was overcome with sadness as she traced the tragic events. The intransigence of the *émigrés*, the aristocrats who had abandoned their country in the hope of restoring the monarchy with foreign help, matched the fanatic excesses of the republicans. The creation of fear and suspicion of both republicans and royalists alike precipitated the country into the arms of Napoleon at the time of the coup d'état (18th, 19th *Brumaire*). "I wept not over liberty, for it never existed in France, but over the hope of that liberty."[12]

Much of Volume II is devoted to her father's ideas and his critique of the various constitutions up to Napoleon's arrival on the scene. It is Necker who prophesied failure because the Revolution had triumphed over justice, "which destroys those who overturn it." The remedy for popular passions is to be found not in despotism but in the sovereignty of the law, in the conciliation of opposing forces. This was always the basis of her thought.

She criticizes English policy following the Napoleonic Wars.

She appeals for leniency for the French people, though they knew what their government was doing, and they were thus not relieved of guilt. She wrote: "Of what use is the law of retaliation in general, and above all, the law of retaliation exercised against a nation? Is a people today what it was yesterday? Does not a new and innocent generation come to replace that which has been found guilty? If it be hardly practicable in a question of political opinion to try one man with equity, how then can a nation be tried?"[13] Mme de Staël would teach us what we in the West have learned today, that former enemies must be treated as equals.

Bonaparte

Of Napoleon she wrote: "Bonaparte is not a man only, but also a system; and if he were right, the human species would no longer be what God has made it . . . his twofold dexterity consisted in the art of dazzling multitudes and corrupting individuals."[14] "It is impossible to deny, in some respects, the truth of what Bonaparte said afterwards: 'I found the crown of France on the ground and picked it up,' but it was the French nation which required to be raised."[15]

In Chapter 8, Volume II, of *Considerations*, Mme de Staël claims that she discovered sooner than others the designs of tyranny in Napoleon. Actually it was some time before she became hostile to him. Her hope was to influence him as she had influenced many, such as Talleyrand, Narbonne, Benjamin Constant, and others. She knew Napoleon read Ossian and the philosophers. She pictured him romantically during the first conquests. She wrote to him, committing in one letter the great mistake of referring to his marriage to Josephine as "An unnatural union for such a genius" (to an insignificant little Créole).[16] Gautier claims that the conflict between Napoleon and Germaine was one of domination by one or the other; that at first he was friendly but disliked her type of woman. Bonaparte knew her past relations with the government and feared her reckless, dominating personality and her power of thought.

Mme de Staël makes the point that Bonaparte "Was vexed that I should be the only writer of reputation in France who had published books during his reign without making any mention of his gigantic existence, and at last with inconceivable rage he suppressed my work on Germany."[17]

Bonaparte's Empire

For his empire he created kingdoms, fiefs, in conquered countries, and restored the trappings of the old *régime*. What did he offer Europe? Himself, and highroads for his troops, monuments to his glory, and some remains of constitutional government such as the improvement of jurisprudence, public education, and the encouragement of the sciences. Wasn't this a poor recompense for the degrading yoke, the loss of liberty, she asked. Was a nation made to serve as his pedestal? She generously admitted France's debt to Napoleon for its art museums, for the beautification of Paris, for the construction of good roads and canals.

She was not qualified to judge his military skill, she said. He had astonishing victories and was a man "in many respects of transcendent genius."[18] Battles, however, must be judged like any other events or enterprises in the world, "according to the goodness of the cause and the utility of the result."[19] Otherwise there would be neither liberty nor morality in the world.

She has a certain degree of praise for Bonaparte: "Every time that I heard him speak, I was struck by his superiority, yet it was not that of a man cultivated by study or society."[20] At one point she wrote of Bonaparte: "I felt in his soul a cold, sharp-edged sword which froze the wound which it inflicted. I perceived in his understanding a profound irony, from which nothing great or beautiful, not even his own glory, could escape; for he despised the nation whose suffrages he wished, and no spark of enthusiasm was mingled with his desire of astonishing the human race."[21] Only war suited him. He even looked best on a horse.

Bonaparte's Character

Bonaparte, she thought, was not sanguinary but indifferent to the fate of men in the pursuit of his ends. He believed that men were all governed by self-interest. He laughed at enthusiasm, "But it was when there remained nothing more for him to conquer in Europe that Fate seized upon him, and made him fall with as much rapidity as he had risen."[22] He had grown fat in prosperity. He had reduced men to an echo of himself and no longer got the true facts of a situation.

After Napoleon was defeated she refused to join those who calumniated him. She judged him as a public man, according to what he did for "the prosperity, the enlightenment and morality of nations." His persecution of her did not influence her opinion; in fact she had to resist being influenced by the feeling she had of his extraordinary genius.[23]

Constitutional Charter of 1814

From Part V on, Mme de Staël was not able to revise her work. The chapters contain, however, her thoughtful analysis of government and its elements. Perhaps the most interesting comments she made were those concerning the Constitutional Charter of June 4, 1814, under Louis XVIII, after the abdication of Napoleon. She protested against the King's granting the Charter by decree; it should have been the people who required it of the King. Almost all its articles in support of liberty had been proposed by Necker in 1789 to Louis XVI.[24] Unfortunately, the ministers of Louis XVIII reduced the liberty of the press and religious toleration and continued the new aristocracy.

The One Hundred Days

Of Napoleon's escape from Elba, March 6, 1815, she wrote: "The march from Cannes to Paris is one of the greatest conceptions of audacity that can be cited in history."[25] She was frightened, however, by the event. Napoleon reassured her and asked for her cooperation. She could not believe that his conversion to the principles of liberty was sincere and remained aloof. "His final defeat was a great moral lesson to the world. Such egotism must go down in defeat."[26] "Time will bring to light the principal traits of his character; and those who are willing to admire every extraordinary man, have a right to think him such."[27]

Final Chapters

The final chapters of *Considerations,* as she has sketched them, treat of England, its prosperity, its spirit of liberty, its religion and morals, its society, and its conduct of government. Her admiration is not entirely unqualified, however. She felt that the Irish situation demanded change. She admired the English for abolishing the slave trade for their colonial government, as in India. She protested against the British burning of Washington, D.C.: "It was not war-like establishments that were destroyed, but peaceful edifices, sacred to national representation, to public instruction, to the transplantation of arts and sciences into a country recently overspread with forests, and conquered only by the labor of men."[28]

She expressed her admiration of America as follows: "What is there more honorable for mankind than this new world, which has established itself without the prejudices of the old; this new world where religion is in all its fervor; without needing the support of the state to maintain it; where the law commands by the respect which it inspires, without being enforced by military power?"[29] Her faith in the New World provides food for thought today, over one hundred and seventy-five years later.

Since Mme de Staël spent the last months of her exile in England while the battles of the Coalition were in progress on the Continent, what she observed and discussed was fresh in her mind when she wrote *Considerations.* She wrote from personal observation and conviction.

Mme de Staël's last chapter is entitled "Love of Liberty." In it she discussed the opponents of liberty, who in every country are always enemies of knowledge and intelligence. She gave good warning to the men of politics to come after her. Three groups are named as these enemies: (1) the aristocrats convinced of the necessity of a monarchy; (2) the men disgusted and disillusioned by the French Revolution; (3) the Bonapartists and Jacobins who refused to take conscience as a guide in politics.[30] Those who serve freedom are the chosen portion, the *élite,* of the human race. In every country they agree on the abolition of the slave trade, on the liberty of the press, on religious toleration. "Jefferson thinks as La Fayette; La Fayette as Wilberforce."[31] "It is in the soul, not in the calculation of self-interest, that the principles of liberty are founded."[32] Here is her internationalism. The principles of freedom are the same the world over.

Here, as in everything she wrote, there can be seen both the power of her intellect and the impulse of her affections. In her character the two were inseparable, a sort of marriage of reason and enthusiasm, which she herself recognized. It is certain that Mme de Staël developed many of her ideas on literature, science, and government from other minds produced by the Enlightenment—from the study of Montesquieu, Condorcet, and others—but she used these ideas for her own purpose. That purpose was "to explain all literature [both imaginative and analytical] by its relation to social institutions."[33] That purpose was also to help guide Europe, and especially France, into the Republican era.

She was a true cosmopolitan, and her voice was raised in the cause of humanity and freedom everywhere. She stood on the threshold of the Romantic era. Indeed, she has something of real value to say to us today.

CHAPTER 13

Influence

TO CONSIDER the influence and importance of Mme de Staël let us first summarize the ideas she interpreted and originated. These ideas matured from the early enthusiasm for Jean-Jacques Rousseau to the critical consideration of literatures and government and their relationship in her later works. Not that she ever lost the Rousseauistic influence expressed in her passionate affections, her sentimental expansiveness and confidence in the goodness of man, for this was her own nature, but she repudiated Rousseau's pessimism and intolerance and left his ideas of morality and God to arrive in her later years close to the Christian faith, though refusing its dogmas.

Mme de Staël brings to the unsettled and changing world of today an uplifting concept of the historical progress of man. Even in the midst of the staggering holocaust of the French Revolution she held to her faith in man's perfectibility, in the power of enlightened thought to lift man above the morass of violence, selfishness, and hatred. Her voice was constantly raised against all phases of fanaticism, often at great cost to herself. She spoke for tolerance, conciliation, humanity, and against despotism in government and its corrupting influence under Napoleon. She held great ideas to be indestructible and to belong to all nations.

Her book, *Of Literature Considered in Its Relations to Social Institutions,* presents the idea that literature and a nation's character and political institutions are interrelated. Mme de Staël believed that political institutions, especially those of a free people, influence its literature. She used her study of history and of the literatures of nations from the Greeks and Romans up to her day to prove this relation. In this sense she developed the study of comparative literature. For Mme de Staël freedom to think and to express thought, the highest quality of man, shaped the continuous progress of man. Thus, to enlightened, educated men belonged the leadership of a nation. Literature in her eyes was also a source of uplift and comfort to the depressed and discouraged.

Mme de Staël was a true cosmopolitan. She spent much of her life outside France, in Germany, Italy, England, Sweden, Switzerland, and Russia. By nature she was receptive to new ideas, curious of other cultures and literatures which she interpreted and described with keen analysis in *Germany*, and *Ten Years of Exile*. The excitement of discussion with friends, Benjamin Constant, Barante, Talleyrand, Narbonne, Wilhelm Humboldt, and a host of others, some in foreign countries—Schiller and Goethe in Germany, Mackintosh, and Wilberforce in England— inspired in her new concepts that she believed would enrich the French as well as others. Since conversation was her forte and conversation by its rapid crossfire of ideas does not lend itself to careful style and depth of analysis, her writings have not the careful brilliance of Chateaubriand. "Her finest books were never written."[1] It was always ideas, concepts that occupied her mind.

Fiction, Literature *and* Germany

What were these new concepts? In her *Essay on Fiction*, in *Literature*, in *Germany*, and in many of her prefaces she sets forth a new poetic system, one free from the imitation of the past, free from rules and based on the expression of the heart, on sentiment not artificiality. In this system she repudiates the use of irony which withers the soul. Enthusiasm, revealed by the heart and confirmed by reason, and faith in progress—these form her credo.

She divided literature into that of the north and that of the south; her emphasis on, and preference for, the north, the qualities of free, Romantic imagination, of melancholy and native poetic inspiration rather than on the careful form and transplanted subjects of the classical writers influenced her descendants. She was the first to use the term Romantic. The concept of her mission to wake up the French to the ideals of literary freedom and lyrical self-expression was original. She introduced international characters, the English Oswald, the French d'Erfeuil, the Italian Corinne in her novel *Corinne*. She set out her theories: (1) The novel should include in its portraiture of characters not only the subject of love but also other passions—hatred, avarice, jealousy, and so on—and should have a moral and philosophical thought hidden in the text. (2) Criticism should be directed not only to the analysis of the faults of a work but should reveal its beauties (this is echoed by Chateaubriand in his *Mélanges Littéraires* and it came to be the basis of the literary criticism of the nineteenth century). (3) The soul of poetry is enthusiasm, the lyric expression of the poet's own feelings of love, of the infinite, nature, and death. (4) Genius should not be the blind slave of taste. (5) Most important of all, men should be freed by education from their superstitions and prejudices, for only free enlightened men are capable of true progress. It is authoritarianism in government and religion which obstruct this. She emphasized the progress of the sciences but warned that moral progress must accompany them. She suggested the possibility of politics becoming a science, the study of which is today an accepted fact.

Considerations

Considerations, which, in Sainte-Beuve's estimation sealed Mme de Staël's place in posterity, presented many political ideas which have become commonplace today. Freedom, she felt, and attempted to prove in her analysis of history through the ages, was a steady leaven, raising the masses upward from the time of the struggling burgesses to the rise of the Third Estate. The French historians Guizot, Michelet, and Lamartine have since followed her liberal theory.

Such excesses as those of the Revolution could be avoided only by education, a truth emphasized at the present time in the civil rights struggle, and that of the emerging nations.

She emphasized the value of the study of foreign languages, another idea which Americans are accepting and implementing in their schools today.

She has been praised and sometimes blamed for her brilliant generalizations and by some critics taken to task for her errors of scholarly detail. Her work, however, was inspired by enthusiasm, and was created in the heat of the stimulating exchange of ideas with the brilliant minds around her. No woman of her time, or since, has so well represented her age or more deeply influenced those around her and their descendants.

The cause of liberty, the civic and social freedoms for which she fought are still in question. But women of intelligence and understanding have their rightful place in many countries today. She idealized America, born, she thought, without the prejudices and intolerance of the Old World. Were she alive today she might caution us about too great haste in our efforts to remake society. Wise with the experience of a lifetime of upheaval she brings to the student of today a lucid and dynamic presentation of ideas and problems which will engage his sympathy as well as his intellectual interest.

The question is asked, "Why are her political and social views so relevant to us today?" To quote Morroe Berger: "I think because the eighteenth century's ethics and rationalism have not yet been superseded as ideals; its distillation of the accumulated knowledge about social life remains largely valid. Madame de Staël spoke for rationality, also for feeling. She saw European civilization as a whole, not in order to oppose it to other civilizations, but to give it its place among them. She did not believe that Europe's energy, integrity and greatness depended upon injustices like slavery and imperialism, or that the end of these injustices would reduce Europe's cultural potentialities. She was often wrong, but never weak. She often failed, but was never dispirited for very long, or vindictive at all. She saw the defeat of reason many times, but never doubted it as an ideal."[2]

Influence on Romanticists

Let us examine in more detail the influence of Mme de Staël on the writers of the Romantic movement. Although her influence on political thought made her home in 1816 the nucleus of the great liberal party which was the honor of nineteenth-century France, much more emphasis is placed on her influence on literature. Over the years she had introduced to one another either in her *salon*, or as guests at her home in Coppet, or in her writings, the prominent men of literature, of science, and of philosophy from the Continent, from England, and from America. Her purpose was to exchange and stimulate ideas, to break down the walls of tradition and national ignorance and thereby reinvigorate thought, literary thought in particular. She succeeded so well that *Germany* became, in the words of one critic, the bible of the Romanticists for thirty years.[3]

When *Germany* appeared in France in 1814 it created a furor. There were four editions by 1819. For many of the French, with the armies of occupation covering their land, it was difficult to reverse the current of influence which up to that time had been from France to Europe.[4] She was bitterly attacked for lacking national pride, but it was this very pride in France that had made her open the doors of thought to a rebirth of French literature.

Poets and dramatists were, however, waiting, eager and ready, to receive her ideas. Lamartine read *Germany* and the essay on *The Influence of the Passions*. He followed in her footsteps in his journey to Italy and his *Meditations*, which appeared in 1820 shortly after her death, dealt with subjects and in a manner which showed her influence, the Roman Coliseum, immortality, melancholy love. In one of his poems he speaks directly to her: "Mais mon âme à Coppet s'envole vers tes rives." The passionate heroine of *Jocelyn* is certainly related to Delphine. His poem, "Bonaparte," with its strong words of condemnation, reflects Mme de Staël's description of Napoleon's character in *Ten Years of Exile*. In America *Germany* inspired many writers to study German culture, including Margaret Fuller, George Bancroft, Emerson, and Longfellow. Victor Hugo took her ideas and enlarged and reshaped them in his *Préface de Cromwell*—a manifesto of Romanticism.

Préface de Cromwell

It is interesting to compare the ideas of Mme de Staël with Hugo's clear-cut and dynamic manifesto. He breathes into it a feeling which is certainly reminiscent of her exuberance. Like Mme de Staël, Hugo makes a survey of the literature of civilization under the titles of the Three Ages of Man: the Primitive, with lyrical treatment of God, of the soul, and Creation (Genesis); that of Antiquity, with the epics such as Homer's and men as giants; and finally that of the Moderns, which begins with Christianity. He speaks as she did of the Middle Ages with the development of Christian melancholy and scholasticism (St.

Augustine). Christianity, wrote Hugo, brings truth to poetry. The ugly exists beside the beautiful, evil beside the good, shadow beside the light, the grotesque as the reverse of the sublime.

From the mixture of the grotesque and the sublime is born "modern genius, so complex, so varied in its forms, so inexhaustible in its creations and contrary to the uniform simplicity of the genius of the ancients." As did Mme de Staël he admits only one unity of the Classicists' three, that of action, which, he says, does not preclude secondary actions related to the central one. The main emphasis is in nature and truth and the subjects chosen should bring history to life and create poetry. Mme de Staël used other words, but her thought was similar.

Hugo continues with the theater in which he says the inner man should be portrayed in asides and the exterior man in speech and action. Local color should be the heart of each work. The monotony of the Alexandrine line should be changed by the variation of the caesura and enjambement. The basis of dramatic style should be a verse which is "libre, franc, loyal, osant tout dire sans pruderie, tout exprimer sans recherche." It is evident that much of this was anticipated by the literary criticism of Mme de Staël. Insisting as she always did on good taste, the preservation of decency in the action and the language, she might have said to Hugo: "Your ideas are good. I'm glad to see new creativity, new forms take shape but let's be careful of extremes and exaggeration. Let me observe your works." To her reason, morality, tolerance, and humanity were the foundations of true liberty in art as in life. She had seen good ideas carried to harmful extremes in real life during the Revolution.

Hugo's *Odes et Ballades*, his *Légende des Siècles*, his novels, *Notre Dame de Paris*, *Quatre-Vingt-Treize*, his dramas, *Hernani*, *Ruy Blas*, *Les Burgraves*, to mention a few; the lyric stanzas of Musset's *Nuits* and even the somber self-revelation of Vigny's philosophic poems and his novel, *Cinq-Mars* reflect her influence. Balzac also recognized his debt to her in his *Comédie Humaine*. He esteemed her as "the spokesman of her age," along with such odd bedfellows as Tacitus, Luther, Calvin, Voltaire, Rousseau, and others.

That her reputation had spread to America we have the touching testimony in George Ticknor's *Life, Letters and Journals*, published in Boston in 1876. Ticknor was twenty-four years old when he went to Europe after abandoning a career as a lawyer for the study of literature. He spent some years of study at the University of Göttingen and in travels through France, Italy, and England. He met most of the men of letters of these countries who knew Mme de Staël; he was entertained by her family, and he was most anxious to meet this woman who was so highly considered by men of culture and influence everywhere. On his return to the United States he was given the professorship of modern languages at Harvard University where he taught for many years.

In his Journal of May 11, 1817, he records his visit to Mme de Staël in Paris.[5] "At last I have seen Madame de Staël!" (She had been too ill to receive him on a previous occasion.) He notes the sparkle in her eyes as she speaks to him despite her great physical weakness. "Il ne faut pas me juger de ce que vous voyez ici. Ce n'est pas moi; ce n'est que l'ombre de ce que j'étais il y a quatre mois." She speaks to him as an American. "You are the avant-garde of the human race. You are the future of the world." Thinking that he was on his way home to America, she said, "You will soon be home and I, I, too, shall be there."

Albertine, who was present, hid her feelings of grief at this statement, and Ticknor hastened to assure Germaine that she would soon be better and back at Coppet, to which the answer was, "God grant that it may be possible."

Two months later on the day so important to Mme de Staël's faith and hope, July 14, the day of French Independence, her body lay quiet in death,[6] but her thought continues even today to invigorate the hopes of man for a better, more compassionate world.

Germaine's great gift was enthusiasm, which illuminated her brilliant flow of ideas and inspired those around her. Her faults were many, but her virtues far outweighed them. Her faith in man's progress and her firm hold on the torch of freedom were her legacy to our generation.

Notes and References

Chapter One

1. Madame de Staël, *Germany*, with notes and appendices by O. W. Wright (New York: Derby and Jackson, 1861), Vol. II, p. 77.

2. Lady Blennerhasset, *Madame de Staël, Her Friends and Her Influence in Politics and Literature* (London: Chapman and Hall, 1889), Vol. I, p. 184.

3. J. Christopher Herold, *Mistress to an Age* (Copyright, 1958, reprinted by permission of the publishers, The Bobbs-Merrill Company, Inc.), p. 26.

4. Blennerhasset, Vol. I, p. 398.

5. Herold, p. 12.

6. *Ibid.*, p. 14.

7. *Ibid.*, pp. 4, 5.

8. *Ibid.*, p. 6.

9. *Ibid.*, p. 6.

10. Margaret Goldsmith, *Madame de Staël, Portrait of a Liberal in the Revolutionary Age* (London, New York and Toronto: Longmans, Green & Co., 1938), pp. 4, 5.

11. Necker de Saussure, *Oeuvres Complètes de la Baronne Madame de Staël,* "Notice sur le caractère et les écrits" (Paris: Treutel and Wurtz, 1820), p. 23.

12. Goldsmith, p. 9.

13. Necker de Saussure, p. 24.

14. David Glass Larg, *Madame de Staël: Her Life as Revealed in Her Work 1766-1800. Biographical Study of a Mind and Soul,* translated by Veronica Lewis (New York: Alfred A. Knopf, 1926), p. 7.

15. Goldsmith, p. 23.

16. Albert Leon Guerard, *France* (Ann Arbor, Michigan: The University of Michigan Press, 1959), p. 224.

17. *Ibid.*, p. 224.

18. Herold, p. 41.

19. Goldsmith, p. 18.

20. *Ibid.*, p. 19.

21. *Ibid.*, p. 21.
22. Guerard, p. 224.

Chapter Two

1. Pierre de Lacretelle, *Madame de Staël et les Hommes* (Paris: Grasset, 1939), p. 15.
2. Herold, p. 50.
3. *Ibid.*, p. 60.
4. *Ibid.*, pp. 60-61.
5. *Ibid.*, p. 61.
6. Lacretelle, pp. 24, 25.
7. *Ibid.*, p. 25.
8. *Ibid.*, p. 28.
9. Herold, p. 68.
10. Abel Stevens, *Madame de Staël, A Study of Her Life and Times, the First Revolution and the First Empire* (New York: Harper and Bros., 1881), p. 95.
11. Blennerhasset, Vol. I, p. 151.
12. Goldsmith, p. 43.
13. Albert Sorel, *Madame de Staël* (London: T. Fisher Unwin, 1892), p. 23.
14. Blennerhasset, Vol. I, p. 110.
15. Sainte-Beuve, *Portraits de Femmes* (Paris: Gamier Frères, 1876), p. 91.
16. Larg, p. 60.
17. *Ibid.*, p. 61.
18. Sainte-Beuve, p. 92.
19. Larg, pp. 95, 96.
20. Oeuvres Complètes, *Lettres sur les Ecrits et le caractère de Rousseau, Lettre VI*, p. 101.
21. *Ibid.*, p. 24 (*Lettre II*).

Chapter Three

1. Stevens, pp. 46, 47.
2. *Considerations on the Principal Events of the French Revolution*, Vol. I, p. 60. Edited by the Duc de Broglie and the Baron de Staël (New York: James Eastburn and Co., 1818).
3. Guerard, p. 231.
4. *Ibid.*, p. 231.
5. Goldsmith, p. 52.
6. Levèque, André, *Histoire de la Civilisation française* (New York: Holt, Rinehart and Winston, 1949), p. 300. *The Queen's Necklace,*

Frances Mossiker, Simon and Schuster, N. Y., 1961, tells the whole story in detail.

7. *Considerations*, Vol. I, p. 92.

8. Goldsmith, p. 54.

9. Blennerhasset, Vol. I, pp. 274, 275.

10. De Tocqueville, Alexis, *The Old Regime and the Revolution* (New York: Harper Bros., 1856), translated by John Bonner, p. 170.

11. *Ibid.*, p. 249.

12. *Considerations*, Vol. I, pp. 108, 109.

13. *Ibid.*, p. 109.

14. *Ibid.*, p. 111.

15. *Ibid.*, p. 120.

16. *Ibid.*, p. 118.

17. *Ibid.*, p. 120.

18. Bella Duffy, *Madame de Staël* (London: W. H. Allen & Co., 1887), p. 71.

19. *Considerations*, Vol. I, pp. 162, 163.

20. *Ibid.*, p. 163.

21. François A. M. Mignet, "The French Revolution from 1789-1815" (in Vol. X, *History of Nations*), p. 55. Explanatory note on the revolutionary clubs, hotbeds of discussion for the factions directing the Revolution. They were known by the name of their meeting place, usually some former monastery. "Les Feuillants" was composed of the moderate thinkers, one of which was La Fayette. The Cordeliers were represented by radicals, such as Desmoulins, Marat, and Danton, who was also a Jacobin. The radical Jacobins were a sort of octopus, with groups all over the country. The Girondists were so called because many members came from Bordeaux, Gironde. The Montagnards were a determined radical group, so called from their seats highest up in the Assembly. Guerard, pp. 274, 253.

22. Guerard, p. 238.

23. *Considerations*, Vol. I, p. 138.

24. Mignet, p. 56.

25. *Ibid.*, pp. 64, 65.

26. *Considerations*, Vol. I, p. 149.

27. *Ibid.*, p. 150.

28. Guerard, p. 241.

29. *Ibid.*, p. 241.

30. *Considerations*, Vol. I, p. 159.

31. *Ibid.*, pp. 202, 207.

32. Guerard, p. 243.

33. *Considerations*, Vol. I, p. 264.

34. *Ibid.*, pp. 266-67.

35. Goldsmith, p. 93.

Chapter Four

1. Herold, pp. 63, 64.
2. *Ibid.*, p. 94.
3. Germaine de Staël, *Lettres à Narbonne* (Paris: Librairie Galli-mard, 1960), Introduction, p. 16.
4. Blennerhasset, Vol. I, p. 459.

Gouverneur Morris was representative of the newly born American government. He was royalist in sympathies, visited Madame's *salon* twice a month, differed with her on the power of the Constitution in 1791, even wrote the king a *mémoire* of his ideas. At one time he made a draft for a plan of French government and general principles to accompany it. *Life of Gouverneur Morris* (Jared Sparks, Boston: Gray & Bowen, 1932), p. 364.

He wrote, concerning the riotous day of June 20 when the King was forced to put on the red bonnet: "The Constitution has this day, I think, given its last groan." (*Ibid.*, p. 375.)

He foresaw disaster for the French. Through Morris and an agent Necker purchased lands in northeastern Pennsylvania, and Mme de Staël bought some 23,000 acres in St. Lawrence County, New York, near Morris' own lands. She considered making a trip there in 1802-3. He wrote her a plan for a summer residence there, and a winter residence in Philadelphia or New York. After her death Gustave sold her lands.

5. *Considerations*, Vol. I, p. 295.
6. Blennerhasset, Vol. I, pp. 210-12.
7. *Assignats* and Oath of the Federation. In 1789 the State, threatened with bankruptcy, looked upon the enormous properties held by the Church as a means of rescue. The clergy were no longer a separate order. Their property was nationalized, and funds were set aside to support all the priests working for the religious needs of the people. The remainder was made the basis for the issue of *assignats*, or mortgage notes, bearing interest. The clergy was required to take the Loyalty Oath to the Constitution, an oath which the Pope forbade. This was the cause of cruel persecutions and rebellion. Guerard, pp. 245, 246. Madame de Staël censured this step of the government severely. *Considerations*, Vol. I, p. 277.
8. *Considerations*, Vol. I, pp. 304, 311.
9. *Ibid.*, pp. 302-8.
10. *Ibid.*, p. 308.
11. *Ibid.*, p. 309.
12. *Lettres à Narbonne*, No. 145, p. 444.

13. Blennerhasset, Vol. II, p. 179.
14. Herold, p. 126.
15. *Lettres à Narbonne,* No. 134, p. 403.
16. *Notice, Oeuvres Complètes,* Vol. I, pp. ccxxiv, ccxlii-cclv (Ed., 1820). It is interesting here to note Mme de Staël's relations to her children, as related by her cousin, Mme Necker de Saussure. She was loved and respected by her children. She believed that passionate demonstrations were bad for children, and she felt a sort of maternal *pudeur* in expressing her feelings to Auguste. She reprimanded them for their faults and exposed her own to them. She cared for them tenderly in illness and was anxious in regard to the effect her own decisions would have on them. "I presented life as it is to my children and used no hypocrisy or affectation." She took pleasure in the odd sayings of her young children but did not let them become selfish and conceited. The boys had tutors, but Albertine received her education from her mother. Albertine wrote to Mme de Saussure of the joy she had as a twelve-year-old when her mother conversed with her as equal to equal.
17. *Lettres à Narbonne,* Introduction, p. 24.
18. Herold, p. 165.
19. *Considerations,* Vol. I, p. 337.
20. *Oeuvres Complètes* (ed., Lefèvre, Paris: 1858), Vol. I, p. 59.
21. *Ibid.,* p. 61.
22. *Ibid.,* p. 64.
23. Sainte-Beuve, pp. 98-100.
24. *Oeuvres Complètes* (ed., Lefèvre, Paris: 1853), Vol. I, p. 70.
25. *Ibid.,* p. 71.
26. *Ibid.,* pp. 102-6 (*Réflexions Sur la Paix Intérieure*).
27. *Ibid.,* p. 117.
28. Sainte-Beuve, p. 96.

Chapter Five

1. Herold, p. 135.
2. De Nolde, Elizabeth, *Madame de Staël and Benjamin de Constant* (New York: Putnam and Sons, 1907), p. 21.
3. *Ibid.,* p. 48.
4. Maurice Levaillant, *The Passionate Exiles: Madame de Staël and Madame Récamier* (New York: Farrar, Straus and Cudahy, 1958), p. 100. It is said that *Adolphe* was begun as the story of his relation to Charlotte von Hardenberg but that his affair with Anna Lindsay (1800) entered his thought also. It was Germaine who took over as heroine finally but probably all the women whom Benjamin loved at different times had a part in the story.

5. Harold Nicolson, *Benjamin Constant* (New York: Doubleday and Co., 1949), p. 153.

6. *Ibid.,* p. 157.

7. Munteano, B., *Les Idées Politiques de Madame de Staël et la Constitution de l'An III* (Paris: Société d'Edition "Belles Lettres," 1931), pp. 43-59.

The Constitution of the Year III was written by the Committee of Eleven, and finished June 23, 1795. It was somewhat reactionary, closed the political clubs; provided age qualification of thirty years and over for members of the Assembly; set up a Corps Législatif of two bodies; the lower, Conseil of Five Hundred, elected by Primary Assemblies; the upper body, The Conseil des Anciens, chosen from and by the Corps Législatif. The Executive was vested in five Directors chosen by the upper body from fifty names proposed by the lower body. It was for "meddling" with this Corps Législatif that Mme de Staël was exiled by the Directory in December, 1795. It was this governmental setup with Barras as chief Director (the five reduced to three directors) which was overthrown by the Bonapartes in 1797.

Among the eleven writing the Constitution were Louvet, La Reveilliere, Boissy d'Anglas, Danou, and Lajuinais, all of whom were guests in Mme de Staël's *Salon,* rue du Bac. Of her influence, read Munteano, B.

8. Herold, p. 177.

9. Goldsmith, p. 160.

10. *Considerations,* Vol. I, p. 388.

11. Wayne Andrews, *Germaine, a Portrait of Madame de Staël-Holstein* (New York: Atheneum, 1963), p. 85

12. Gautier, Paul, *Madame de Staël et Napoléon* (Paris: Plon, 1903), p. 4.

13. The Concordat was the agreement between the French Government and the Holy See, established in 1801 to end the quarrel between the French State and the Vatican. The holdings of church property confiscated under the Revolution were confirmed to the owners but the French government was to pay the salaries of the clergy who were now officials of the State. The appointment of bishops, placed in the hands of the government, had to be confirmed by the pope. Catholicism was the religion of the majority but Protestantism and Judaism had equal status. As Emperor, Napoleon considered himself sovereign over the Church universal with the pope his ecclesiastical lieutenant. Guerard, pp. 267-68.

14. The National Order of the Legion of Honor was founded by

Napoleon in 1802. Originally it had social and political importance with the purpose of establishing a following devoted to the *régime* of Napoleon. Today it is an honor granted for outstanding distinction in various fields. Levèque, p. 352.

15. The *Code Civil* of which Napoleon was very proud and to which he contributed his ideas remains in force today but with many modifications. It was drawn up by a group of experienced jurists. There were over 2000 articles governing in general terms the legal disposition of people and property, such as marriage, divorce, paternity, adoption, inheritance, contracts, etc. It brought order out of the chaos of Roman law and local customs which then reigned in France. Guerard, p. 268.

16. Mignet, p. 460.

Chapter Six

1. Larg., p. 158.
2. *Ibid.*, p. 163.
3. *Oeuvres Complètes* (ed., Lefèvre, Paris: 1858, Vol. I., p. 127.
4. *Ibid.*, Vol. I, p. 128.
5. *Ibid.*, p. 136.
6. *Ibid.*, p. 139.
7. *Ibid.*, p. 141.
8. *Ibid.*, p. 147.
9. *Ibid.*, Vol. II, p. 6.
10. *Ibid.*, p. 6.
11. *Ibid.*, p. 4.
12. *Ibid.*, pp. 30-127.
13. *Ibid.*, p. 46.
14. *Ibid.*, p. 46.
15. *Ibid.*, p. 54.
16. *Ibid.*, p. 55.
17. *Ibid.*, p. 61.
18. *Ibid.*, p. 76.
19. *Ibid.*, p. 79.
20. *Ibid.*, p. 81.
21. *Ibid.*, p. 108.
22. *Ibid.*, p. 116.
23. *Ibid.*, p. 121.
24. *Ibid.*, p. 127.
25. Larg, p. 215.

Chapter Seven

1. Andrews, pp. 81-82.
2. Gautier, p. 34.

3. Andrews, p. 92.
4. Necker de Saussure, *Notice* to *Oeuvres Complètes*, 1820, p. lxxxv.
5. Sainte-Beuve, p. 108.
6. Herold, p. 211.
7. *Oeuvres Complètes* (ed., Lefèvre, Paris: 1858), Vol. II, p. 164.
8. Blennerhasset, Vol. II, pp. 380, 381.
9. Berger, Morroe, *Madame de Staël on Politics, Literature and National Character,* translated and edited by Morroe Berger (New York: Doubleday and Co., 1964), p. 245.
10. *Ibid.*, p. 245; cf. *Oeuvres de Condorcet*, Vol. I, ed. by O'Connor and Arago, 12 vols. (Paris: 1847-49), pp. 539-73.
11. *Oeuvres Complètes* (ed., Lefèvre, Paris: 1853), Vol. II, p. 424.
12. Herold, p. 188.

Chapter Eight

1. De Staël, *Delphine,* translator unnamed (London: J. Mawman, 1803), Preface, Vol. I, p. 6.
2. *Ibid.*, p. 8.
3. *Ibid.*, p. 10.
4. *Ibid.*, p. 6.
5. Sainte-Beuve, p. 127-28.
6. *Delphine*, Vol. V., pp. 114, 115.
7. Necker de Saussure, *Notice* to *Oeuvres Complètes*, 1820-21, p. 103.
8. *Delphine*, Vol. II, p. 7.
9. *Ibid.*, Vol. III, p. 10.
10. *Ibid.*, p. 161-62.
11. *Ibid.*, Vol. IV, p. 129.
12. *Ibid.*, p. 125, 136.
13. *Ibid.*, Vol. II, p. 214.
14. Stevens, p. 267.
15. Stevens, p. 285.

Chapter Nine

1. Grimm was the author of the *Correspondance littéraire,* the most famous newsletter of the age, subscribed to by kings. Meister was a friend of the Neckers. F. H. Jacobi was a German philosopher and friend of Charles Villers.
2. De Pange, Madame la Comtesse, *Madame de Staël et la Découverte de l'Allemagne,* 1929, p. 13.
3. *Ibid.*, p. 14.

4. *Ibid.*, p. 35.
5. *Ibid.*, p. 41.
6. *Ibid.*, p. 43.
7. *Ibid.*, pp. 47-48.
8. Wilson, Robert McNair, *Madame de Staël, High Priestess of Love*, New York: R. M. McBride & Co., 1931, p. 214. Madame de Staël had written to her cousin, Mme Necker de Saussure from Berlin, "Oh, how I'm relying on your promise to take care of my father's health . . . I don't believe I could survive his loss . . . He is part of my memory; partner in every thought. Without him nothing in the past, nothing in the present, nothing in the future. Nothing but despair! It's a fearful thought, for nature certainly did not intend that anyone should love thus another so far advanced beyond her years. But he found means to inspire in me a loving tenderness of so inexpressible a strength that when sometimes I have tried to weaken its influence over me, the result has been merely an enormous increase of that influence."
9. De Pange, p. 72.
10. *Corinne, or Italy,* translated by Isabel Hill (New York: A. L. Burt Co., n. d.), p. 20.
11. *Ibid.*, p. 50.
12. *Ibid.*, p. 54.
13. *Ibid.*, p. 57.
14. *Ibid.*, p. 58.
15. *Ibid.*, p. 65.
16. *Ibid.*, p. 66.
17. *Ibid.*, p. 63.
18. *Ibid.*, pp. 338-42.
19. *Ibid.*, p. 87.
20. *Ibid.*, p. 136.
21. *Ibid.*, p. 3.
22. Sainte-Beuve, p. 155.
23. Herold, p. 312.

Chapter Ten

1. Nicolson, p. 40.
2. *Ibid.*, p. 137.
3. *Ibid.*, p. 195.
4. Forsberg and Nixon, *Mme de Staël and Freedom Today* (Astra Books, New York: 1963), pp. 39-40.
5. Herold, p. 359.
6. *Ibid.*, p. 371.
7. *Oeuvres Complètes* (ed., 1853), Vol. III, Preface, p. 2.

8. Herold, p. 391.
9. *Germany*, p. 22.
10. *Ibid.*, p. 70.
11. *Ibid.*, p. 77.
12. *Ibid.*, pp. 86, 88.
13. *Ibid.*, p. 121.
14. *Ibid.*, "General Observations," p. 24.
15. *Ibid.*, p. 25.
16. *Ibid.*, p. 77.
17. *Ibid.*, p. 81.
18. *Ibid.*, p. 92.
19. *Ibid.*, p. 121.
20. *Ibid.*, p. 125.
21. *Ibid.*, p. 126.
22. *Ibid.*, p. 122.
23. *Ibid.*, p. 146.
24. *Ibid.*, p. 178.
25. *Ibid.*, pp. 177, 178.
26. *Ibid.*, p. 179.
27. *Ibid.*, p. 181.
28. *Ibid.*, p. 183.
29. *Ibid.*, p. 184.
30. *Ibid.*, p. 192.
31. *Ibid.*, p. 196.
32. *Ibid.*, p. 204.
33. *Ibid.*, p. 231.
34. *Ibid.*, p. 249.
35. *Ibid.*, pp. 254-57.
36. *Ibid.*, pp. 262-63.
37. *Ibid.*, p. 360.
38. *Ibid.*, p. 361.
39. *Ibid.*, Vol. II, p. 22.
40. *Ibid.*, p. 24.
41. *Ibid.*, p. 77.
42. *Ibid.*, p. 93.
43. *Ibid.*, Part III, p. 116.
44. *Ibid.*, p. 117.
45. *Ibid.*, p. 118.
46. *Ibid.*, p. 124.
47. *Ibid.*, pp. 128, 129.
48. *Ibid.*, pp. 130, 131.
49. *Ibid.*, pp. 133-34.
50. *Ibid.*, p. 140.
51. *Ibid.*, p. 150.

52. *Ibid.*, p. 153.
53. *Ibid.*, p. 159.
54. *Ibid.*, p. 170.
55. *Ibid.*, p. 171.
56. *Ibid.*, p. 239.
57. *Ibid.*, p. 270.
58. *Ibid.*, p. 272.
59. *Ibid.*, pp. 291-92.
60. *Ibid.*, pp. 294-95.
61. *Ibid.*, pp. 333-36.
62. *Ibid.*, Vol. I, pp. 46-48.
63. *Ibid.*, Vol. II, p. 360.
64. *Ibid.*, p. 360.
65. *Ibid.*, p. 367.
66. *Ibid.*, p. 371.
67. *Ibid.*, p. 376.
68. Goldsmith, p. 220 .

Chapter Eleven

1. Herold, p. 408.
2. Stevens, p. 101.
3. Goldsmith, pp. 230-31.
4. Levaillant, p. 302.
5. *Ten Years of Exile,* no translator named (Treuttel and Wirtz, Treuttel Jr. and Richter, London: 1821), pp. 200, 231.
6. *Ibid.*, pp. 242-43.
7. *Ibid.*, pp. 301-2.
8. *Ibid.*, p. 307.
9. *Ibid.*, pp. 291-97.
10. *Ibid.*, pp. 313, 323.
11. *Ibid.*, p. 329.
12. *Ibid.*, p. 335.
13. *Ibid.*, Vol. II, p. 1.
14. *Ibid.*, pp. 57, 58.
15. *Ibid.*, pp. 145, 146.
16. *Ibid.*, p. 35.
17. *Ibid.*, p. 127.
18. Herold, p. 437.
19. Goldsmith, p. 252.
20. Guerard, p. 279.
21. Wilson, Robert McNair, p. 274.
22. *Ibid.*, p. 274.
23. Goldsmith, p. 256.
24. Herold, p. 469.

25. Chateaubriand, *Mémoires d'Outre-tombe,* Vol. VIII, p. 14.
26. Levaillant, p. 331.
27. Goldsmith, p. 266.

Chapter Twelve

1. *Considerations,* Vol. I, p. 1.
2. *Ibid.,* p. 8.
3. *Ibid.,* p. 8.
4. *Ibid.,* p. 43.
5. *Ibid.,* p. 118.
6. *Ibid.,* p. 157.
7. *Ibid.,* p. 159.
8. *Ibid.,* p. 255.
9. *Ibid.,* p. 283.
10. *Ibid.,* p. 317.
11. *Ibid.,* p. 394.
12. *Ibid.,* Vol. II, p. 8.
13. *Ibid.,* p. 291.
14. *Ibid.,* p. 2.
15. *Ibid.,* Vol. I, p. 404.
16. Gautier, p. 2.
17. *Considerations,* Vol. II, p. 48.
18. *Ibid.,* p. 78.
19. *Ibid.,* p. 79.
20. *Ibid.,* Vol. I, p. 388.
21. *Ibid.,* pp. 388, 389.
22. *Ibid.,* Vol. II, p. 106.
23. *Ibid.,* pp. 113-14.
24. *Ibid.,* p. 148.
25. *Ibid.,* p. 193.
26. *Ibid.,* p. 204.
27. *Ibid.,* p. 205.
28. *Ibid.,* p. 287.
29. *Ibid.,* pp. 287, 288.
30. *Ibid.,* p. 330.
31. *Ibid.,* p. 337. It is interesting here to make note of two English-men whose friendship and ideas were dear to Madame de Staël; William Wilberforce, whose life work was the abolition of slavery and the slave trade, and Sir James Mackintosh who was one of the first to hail the rise of liberty in Europe despite his later disappointment. While serving the British government in India he read Germaine's *Corinne* and found it "a powerful and extraordinary book; full of faults so obvious, as not to be worth enumerating; but of which a single sentence

has excited more feeling, and exercised more reason than the most faultless models of elegance."

It was at the request of Wellington, then English ambassador to France, that Madame de Staël translated for the French people Wilberforce's pamphlet on the cruelty of the slave trade and how to abolish it. In February, 1816, the Congress of Vienna passed a charter for the abolition of the slave trade, which was signed by many nations, including the United States. Unfortunately only England enforced the law and the slave ships continued to transport their sad victims.

32. *Ibid.*, p. 338.
33. Berger, Introduction, p. 30.

Chapter Thirteen

1. Pelissier, p. 51.
2. Berger, Introduction, pp. 88-9.
3. De Pange, p. 146.
4. *Ibid.*, p. 140.
5. Ticknor, *Life, Letters and Journals,* Vol. I, pp. 132-33.
6. The family after Germaine's death.
The disappearance of Germaine's vital spirit left all who had known her intimately with a vacuum in their lives. Benjamin Constant recovered and became a force in the liberal movement in the French government. It has been said that much of what he spoke and wrote he owed to her influence. He died in 1830, survived by Albertine and Alphonse. Rocca's death occurred six months after that of Germaine. His frail son married the granddaughter of Narbonne but died childless at the age of twenty-six.

Auguste de Staël, Germaine's oldest son, married and had a son who survived him by only a few years. Auguste died in 1828. Only Albertine, whom Germaine herself had educated, carried on her mother's spirit. She played an important role in the political and literary society of her time. It was her descendants who became statesmen, historians and scientists.

Selected Bibliography

PRIMARY SOURCES

De Staël, Germaine. *Oeuvres Complètes* de Madame la Baronne de Staël. Publiées par son fils et précedées d'une Notice sur le Caractère et les Ecrits de Madame de Staël par Madame Necker de Saussure. 17 vols. Paris, Treuttel et Wurtz, 1820-21.
This Notice of Mme Necker de Saussure, a cousin who knew her well, is the first biography of Mme de Staël. It is intelligent, comprehensive, and sympathetically critical.
There have been successive editions of her Complete Works, from 1836 and 1838, in 3 vols. For the quotations in this text the 3-volume edition of 1838 (Paris: *chez Lefèvre*) has been used specifically for the following: *Lettres sur Jean-Jacques Rousseau*, her early works, *Essai sur les Fictions*, *Réflexions sur la Paix, adressés à William Pitt et aux Français*, *L'Influence des Passions sur les Individus et les Nations, De la Littérature considérée dans ses rapports avec les Institutions Sociales.*

Works in Chronological Order of Composition or Publication:

1786 *Sophie* or the *Secret Sentiments*, in 3 acts, verse.
1787 *Jane Gray*, tragedy in 5 acts, verse.
1788 *Lettres sur les Ecrits et le Caractère de Jean-Jacques Rousseau.*
1789 *Eulogy of M. de Guibert.*
1793 *Réflexions sur le Procès de la Reine.*
1794 *Réflexions sur la Paix adressées à William Pitt et aux Français.*
1795 *Réflexions sur la Paix Intérieure* (but not published);
Collection of *Epitre au Malheur ou Adèle et Edouard,
Zulma, Mirza, Adélaïde, Histoire de Pauline,
Essai sur les Fictions.*
1796 *L'Influence des Passions sur le Bonheur des Individus et des Nations.*
1801 *De la Littérature considérée dans ses Rapports avec les Institutions Sociales.*

1803   *Delphine; Réflexions sur le But moral de Delphine; Nouveau Dénouement.*

1804   *Caractère de M. Necker.*

1805   *Epître en vers sur Naples.*

1807   *Corinne, ou l'Italie.*

1809   *Préface pour les Lettres et Pensées du Prince de Ligne.*

1806-   *Essais Dramatiques: Agar,* in 3 acts, prose; *La Sunamite,* in 3
1811   acts, prose; *Le Capitaine Kernadec,* comedy in 2 acts, prose;
        La Signora Fantastici, dramatic proverb; *Le Mannequin,* dra-
        matic proverb; *Sapho,* in 5 acts, prose; Articles in the *Bio-
        graphie Universelle, Aspasie, Camöens, Cléopatre* (1811-13)

1813   *De l'Allemagne,* in London; 1814 in Paris.

1813   *Réflexions sur le Suicide,* Stockholm; *Notice sur Lady Jane
        Gray.*

1810-   *Dix Années d'Exil,* published after her death by her son.
1812

1814   *Préface* for and Translation of William Wilberforce's pamphlet,
        "*Abolition of the Slave Trade.*"
        Appeal to the Sovereigns gathered in Paris to abolish the slave
        trade.

1816   *De l'Esprit des Traductions.*

1813-   *Considerations on the Principal Events of the French Revo-
1817   lution,* published by her son and the Marquis de Broglie in
        1817, various translations, written at different times.

Poems: from Goethe, *La Bayadère; The God of India; The Fisher-
        woman.*
        from Schiller, the *Fete of Victory or the Return of the Greeks,*
        and *The Greeting of the Ghost (Le Salut du Revenant);* some
        others from English and Italian.

Lettres à Narbonne. Introduction et notes et Commentaires par
        Georges Solovieff. Préface de la Comtesse de Pange. Paris,
        Librairie Gallimard, 1960.

Translations of Works Used:
        Delphine. Translator unnamed. London: J. Mawman, 1803.
        Corinne, or Italy. Translated by Isabel Hill. New York: A. L.
        Burt and Co., no date given.
        Germany. With notes and appendices by O. W. Wright, AM.
        2 vols. New York: Derby and Jackson, 1861.
        Ten Years of Exile. Published from the original manuscript by
        her son. London: Treuttel and Wurtz. Treuttel, Jr. and Richter,
        1821.
        Considerations on the Principal Events of the French Revolution.
        2 vols. Posthumous work of the Baronness de Staël. No translator

given. New York: James Eastburn and Co., 1818. A new French edition of this was published in 2 vols. by Charpentier, Paris, 1876.

De la Littérature. A critical edition edited by Paul van Tieghem. 2 vols. Paris, Minard and Dros., Geneva, 1959.
De l'Allemagne. Based on M.S. and orginal edition by Comtesse de Pange. Paris, Hachette, 1958-60.

(This list does not exhaust the number of editions, nor does it claim to do so and there is constantly more material coming to light concerning Madame de Staël and those who knew her.)

SECONDARY SOURCES

Blennerhasset, Lady Charlotte. *Madame de Staël, Her Friends and Her Influence in Politics and Literature.* 2 vols. Translated by J. E. Cumming. London: Chapman and Hall, 1889. A most interesting and informative work.
Constant de Rébecque, Benjamin. *Adolphe and the Red Notebook,* with Introduction by Harold Nicolson. A Signet Classic. New York: New American Library of World Literature, 1959.
De Pange, Madame la Comtesse. *Madame de Staël et la Découverte de L'Allemagne.* Paris: Malfère, 1929. Invaluable study for *Germany.*
Gautier, Paul. *Madame de Staël et Napoléon.* Paris: Plon, 1903. A clear analysis of both personalities.
Goldsmith, Margaret. *Madame de Staël, Portrait of a Liberal in the Revolutionary Age.* London, New York and Toronto: Longmans, Green and Company, 1938. Full account, well told.
Herold, Christopher. *Mistress to an Age.* This is the most complete biography. New York: Bobbs Merrill Co. Inc., 1958. It received the National Book Award and was chosen the Book of the Month Selection. We received permission to quote from it.
Larg, David Glass, M. A. *Madame de Staël: Her Life as Revealed in Her Work, 1766-1800.* Biographical Study of a Mind and Soul. Translated by Veronica Lucas. New York: Alfred A. Knopf, 1906.
Levaillant, Maurice. *The Passionate Exiles: Madame de Staël and Madame Récamier.* Translated by Malcolm Barnes. New York: Farrar, Straus and Cudahy, 1958. Brings in Germaine's best friend and another side of her character.
Nicolson, Harold. *Benjamin Constant.* New York: Doubleday and Co., 1949.
Sainte-Beuve, C. A. *Portraits de Femme.* Paris: Garnier Frères, 1876.
Sorel, Albert. *Madame de Staël.* London: T. Fisher Unwin, 1892.

French Edition, Hachette, Paris, no date. One of the best biographies.

Stevens, Abel, LLD. *Madame de Staël, A Study of Her Life and Times, the First Revolution and the First Empire.* 2 vols. New York: Harper and Bros., 1881. A comprehensive study with valuable sidelights.

Other works of interest for specific phases of her life, for the historical background and further appraisal of her influence.

Andrews, Wayne. *Germaine, Portrait of Madame de Staël-Holstein.* New York: Atheneum, 1963. A modern point of view.

Babbitt, Irving. *The Masters of Modern French Criticism.* Boston and New York: Houghton Mifflin, 1912.

Berger, Morroe. *Madame de Staël, on Politics, Literature and National Character.* Translated and edited by Morroe Berger. New York: Doubleday and Co., Inc., 1964.

Birch, Una. *Secret Societies and the French Revolution.* London and New York: John Lane Co., 1911.

Brunetière, Ferdinand. *Histoire de la Littérature Française.* 4 vols. Paris: Delagrave, 1917-19.

Chapman, Elizabeth R. *A Comtist Lover and Other Stories.* With the Delphine of Madame de Staël, pp. 145-183. London: Fisher Unwin, 1886.

Coupland, Reginald. *William Wilberforce, a Narrative.* Oxford: Clarendon Press, 1923.

De Nolde, Baroness Elizabeth. *Madame de Staël and Benjamin Constant.* New York: Putnam and Sons, 1907.

Duffy, Bella. *Madame de Staël.* London: W. H. Allen and Co., 1887.

Faguet, Emile. *Politiques et Moralistes du XIXe Siècle.* Première Série. Paris: Société Française d'Imprimerie et de Librairie, no date.

Forsberg, Roberta and Nixon, J. H. C. *Madame de Staël and Freedom Today.* New York: Astra Books, 1963.

Gribble, Francis Henry. *Madame de Staël and Her Lovers.* New York, London: James Pott and Co., 1907.

Guerard, Albert Leon. *France.* Ann Arbor, Michigan: University of Michigan Press, 1959.

Lacretelle, Pierre de. *Madame de Staël et les Hommes.* Paris: Grasset, 1939.

Lanson, Gustave. *Histoire de la Littérature Française.* Paris: Hachette et Cie., 1912.

Lefèbre, Georges. *Napoléon.* Paris: Presses Universitaires de France, 1953. A clear portrait of the man of destiny.

Selected Bibliography

Mackintosh, James. *Memoirs of the Life of Sir James Mackintosh.* 2 vols. Boston: Little, Brown and Co., 1853.

Mignet, François Auguste Marie. *The French Revolution from 1789-1815.* Volume X of *History of Nations.* Edited with an additional chapter on the Hundred Days by James Westfall Thompson, Ph.D. London: George Bell and Son, 1896.

Pélissier, Georges. *Le Mouvement Littéraire au XIXe Siècle.* Paris: Hachette, 1921.

Rude, George. *The Crowd in the French Revolution.* London: Oxford University Press, 1959.

Saintsbury, George. *History of the French Novel.* 2 vols. London: Macmillan and Co., 1917.

Tallentyre, S. G. *Women of the Salons.* New York: Longmans, Green and Co., 1901.

Thompson, J. M. *Documents of the French Revolution, 1789-94.* Oxford. Oxford University Press, 1933.

Ticknor, George. *Life, Letters and Journal.* Vol. 1. Boston: James R. Osgood and Co., 1876.

Sparks, Jared. *The Life of Gouverneur Morris* with Selections from his correspondence and miscellaneous papers. Vol. 1. Boston: Gray and Bowen, 1832. Sidelight on Mme de Staël from an American diplomat who knew her. Also interesting relation of his opinions concerning the Revolution.

Wilson, Robert McNair. *Germaine de Staël, High Priestess of Love.* New York: Robert M. McBride and Co., 1931. Clear historical background and rather unsympathetic view of her character.

Index

Index

Index
